HABITUALLY GREAT

"**Habitually Great** *shows you a way to gracefully master and change your habits and your life. This is an important and principled examination of how to achieve our individual and collective greatness."*

– STEPHEN R. COVEY, AUTHOR,
THE 7 HABITS OF HIGHLY EFFECTIVE PEOPLE AND *THE LEADER IN ME*

MARK WEINSTEIN

HABITUALLY GREAT
PRODUCTIVITY & TIME MANAGEMENT

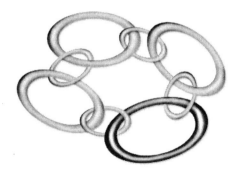

Master The Framework of Your Life

Habitually Great Productivity & Time Management:
Master The Framework of Your Life
Copyright © 2011 by Mark Weinstein

All rights reserved. No part of this book may be used or reproduced in any manner whatsoever without written permission except in the case of brief quotations embodied in critical articles and reviews. For permission, please contact Mark Weinstein at author@habituallygreat.com.

Printed in the United States of America. Distributed by CreateSpace, 7290B Investment Drive, N. Charleston, SC 29418

Visit www.amazon.com or www.createspace.com/3489316
to order additional copies.
For quantity orders please contact Habitually Great, Inc., at:
www.habituallygreat.com

PEAK LIFE HABITS®
Positively Inspiring Success!

Peak Life Habits®, Peak Work Habits®, Habit Blueprint®, and Habitually Great® are registered trademarks. Company and product names mentioned herein are the trademarks or registered trademarks of their respective owners.

ISBN: 1453863427
ISBN: 9781453863428
Library of Congress Control Number: 2010914956

Dedication

This book is dedicated to you. I acknowledge and appreciate the focus you place within your life to be the best you can be. The very fact that you chose this book is a testament to your curiosity, desire, and courage. The only person who can change the world is you, through your powerful intentions and deliberate actions. May the enclosed thoughts, ideas, and practices honorably serve your growth and happiness as you ascend your life. I am proud of you. Carpe Diem!

A Special Thank You

Thank you, Alexia Paul and Plaegian Alexander, two brilliant editors whose superb assistance transformed these pages.

Contents

Introduction   v

Chapter 1
Infuse Your Life with Right Action!   1

Chapter 2
Draw Inspiration from Discipline   7

Chapter 3
Put the "Right Action Momentum Habit" into Play   19

Chapter 4
Get Clear on Your Multiple Roles in Life   29

Chapter 5
Appreciate that Time Is Just Time   33

Chapter 6
Fill Your Buckets of Time with Pure Gold   41

Chapter 7
Schedule Yourself for Habitual Greatness   47

Chapter 8
Employ the Simplest and Most Effective Daily To-Do System   63

Contents (cont'd)

Chapter 9
Prepare for Interruptions
and Banish Distractions — 69

Chapter 10
Carve Out Solitary Work Blocks
with No Interruptions — 81

Chapter 11
Nail Down Your Stop Doing List — 87

Chapter 12
Dream Up Your Start Doing List — 93

Chapter 13
Take On the "Confrontation with
Being Complete Habit" — 97

Chapter 14
Practice Reverse Timeline Scheduling — 103

Chapter 15
Build Teamwork by Mastering
the Art of Delegation — 109

Chapter 16
Be Great at Your Job! — 117

Conclusion:
Putting It All Together — 123

Contents (cont'd)

What To Do Next—In Your Life Take Action To Be Habitually Great	130
What To Do Next—At Work Take Action To Be Habitually Great	132
Appendix A: Peak Life Habits List	136
Appendix B: Limiting Habits List	140
Appendix C: Shifting Habits Chart	142
About the Author	149

Introduction

Have you ever wondered why so many of your New Year's resolutions wither on the vine? Have you made the same resolution(s) two years (or more) in a row? New Year's resolutions are born from inspiration, not discipline. Their aim is virtuous: to achieve a result by changing, breaking, or creating a habit. However, the pathway to their fulfillment runs straight into the walls of your well-established habits in spite of your inspired "in the moment" commitment and clarity of intent. In your personal life or within the life of an organization, the cycle is the same. Here's why: inspiration does not lead to sustained action.

Now for the good news: *discipline leads to inspiration.* That's right. You know that when you have truly applied yourself, whether in school, sports, at work, or in some other venue, success has soon followed. Think back to a time or a success that has felt really good (before your "I'm Not Good Enough Habit," "Confrontation With Success Habit," or other saboteurs jumped in). You were inspired! Notice, though, that the inspiration happened *afterward.* Your discipline, sustained through healthy habits, led to your inspiration, and that is the beauty of the equation.

Habits are the elephants in the room of personal and professional improvement. Habits burrow into our brains so deeply that we fail to see their power and influence even though they are, indeed, huge. They leave their tracks across our lives day after day. We have habits about everything: from fitness, nutrition, relationships, spirituality, accountability, and integrity to how we brush our teeth, sit in chairs, think, and manage our time and productivity. Some are good habits—or *Peak Life Habits*, as I'll refer to them in this book. We could not get through a day without good habits, which could be anything from a "No More Excuses Habit" to a "Healthy Exercise Habit" to a "Leading By Example Habit." There are dozens of admirable patterns you act out in life without ever having to think twice about them.

Unfortunately, these life-enhancing patterns aren't the only habits lurking around. Other habits—what I call *Limiting Habits*—tend to exert a negative influence. Limiting Habits are driven by unconsciously held, forceful beliefs that undercut our performance and our self-presentation at critical junctures in our lives. In the grip of these habits, we are left in the realm of "almost," again and again.

You could be 75 years old or 15 (or any age in between) and—just when you are inches away from winning the gold—still only make it to "almost" because of habits you unwittingly acquired when you were six.

(From this point forward, please note that we will be capitalizing such key terms as Belief, Action, Outcome, Habit, Limiting Habit, Peak Life Habit, and Habit mechanism, as these are central, vital concepts to keep in mind. Also note that, in the *Habitually Great* context, to Shift means to choose proactively to exchange your Limiting Habits for Peak Life Habits.)

Going Beyond Almost

Going beyond "almost" requires us to blast through our *Success Ceilings*. A Success Ceiling is a stationary comfort level, several rungs below the penthouse, a cap on how successful we are willing to be in a certain part of life. We may fear the accountability that comes along with reaching a heightened level of success, so we remain at a lower point instead of breaking through the ceiling to a higher level. We can recognize our arrival at a Success Ceiling when we see ourselves self-sabotaging, or becoming distracted or complacent.

Within the shadow of a Success Ceiling are Limiting Habits such as the "Avoid Accountability Habit," Waiting For The Right Time Habit," "Procrastination Habit," and others that determinedly hold us back. Often there is a limiting Belief wedged underneath those Habits about our capabilities, worthiness, relationships, finances, health, etc.

Limiting Habits are excellent diversions. They give us an excuse to avoid what we don't want to face: accountability for our own successes and failures. They create vicious cycles that keep us stuck at "almost." They perpetuate nagging dissatisfactions, those perpetual "good"s rather than "great"s that bar us from our ultimate lives. They keep us in familiar distress instead of allowing us to be fully satisfied with becoming everything we can be. Limiting Habits are the ones that remain fully intact despite all the breakthrough and self-improvement workshops, books, and therapy. They come from our families of origin and from our early experiences and keep us from sustaining goals and successes even if we are able to attain them momentarily.

Companies, organizations, and sports teams have Success Ceilings, too, where they get "good enough" and then become smug and myopic. Over time, their competitors, the ones who are not satisfied with "good," eclipse them.

The lesson here for both individuals and organizations: when it seems easier to derail than to push forward, take note. Limiting Habits are now running the show.

The text, tools, and exercises presented in the following pages are based on the unique Habitually Great system and will teach you how to recognize your Limiting Habits and Shift them to Peak Life Habits. By doing so you will ascend the ranks of happy, successful people and organizations that focus on who they are and what they intend to become. They are in Action at the right place and the right time, just like they were in Action in the days, months, and years before that "right time." From the outside, their Outcomes—getting the gold, the girl, the guy, making an important contribution, creating the life of their dreams, becoming industry, not-for-profit, academic, or athletic leaders—may look like a lucky break or even a miracle, yet it is simply what they've already promised themselves; success through accountable Action.

The Links to Your Habits

If our Habits determine our successes and failures, then the surest way to achieve our dreams is to Shift our Habits. Our Habit mechanism—the underlying Habits that run us—is best pictured as a chain comprising a Belief, an Action, an Outcome, and the resulting Habit, as well as the unspoken connections between all four components.

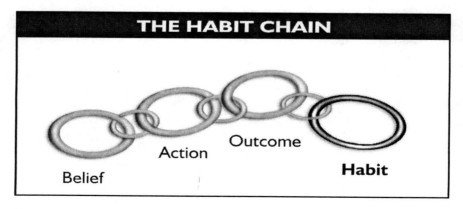

You've heard of a whole being more than the sum of its parts? A Habit Chain is both a whole and the sum of its parts—it is a way of seeing that the whole Habit is in fact the sum of the parts of which it is composed. The Habits you experience every day are the final products of these sticky chains.

Dozens of these Habit Chains operate your behavior and feelings, controlling you like puppet masters. Some of them work in your favor, for instance, allowing you not to take the receptionist's bad mood personally, and in so doing, to stay upbeat with your colleagues. Some Habit Chains work against you, say, when you let an internal voice of second-guessing send you into a tailspin of procrastination. Every single time a Habit guides your Actions, it starts with one of your Beliefs (even though you may not even be conscious of the Belief), and then moves toward an Action that produces an Outcome. If you imagine each Habit as being a mini iceberg, the 10% emerging from the water is the Habit. The other 90% is submerged in your subconscious, in your automatic Beliefs and expectations about the world and other people. So if you've pretty much been running on auto-pilot up till now, this book will help you get back in the driver's seat and show you how to take back over the controls.

It Takes Action, Not Passion, to Succeed

Greatness requires discipline and persistence, not passion. Here's why. We've all experienced times, sometimes even days, weeks, or months, when we feel the blahs, the lack of motivation and passion. An important way to generate momentum is to stay in Action. Have you ever had those moments where you'd lost your mojo, and yet you put yourself into Action and worked your way through your malaise and into a big smile of satisfaction? Passion and inspiration are the Outcomes. Those are unshackled *Habitually Great* moments!

There is nothing revolutionary about scheduling, staying in Action, and following through. The catapult to habitual greatness is in cutting the chains that have stopped you in the past and getting all the way to the checkered flag of completion and success. That's the breakthrough—keeping on and not stopping, no matter what. That is why great athletes and teams *are* great: because they practice, over and over and over again. They practice with purpose and intention. Those practices and drills are scheduled; they are not random, because they play to win! They preemptively work on circumventing anything that could get in the way, like Limiting Habits. Everything is about good and bad Habits, no matter what the endeavor; whether it's how you kick a ball, how you study, how you communicate, how you love, how you think, or how you work. You decide what your trophy case will display and what is important for you to master and feel joyful about. Your Habits will either be in the way or get you all the way.

Growing beyond your comfort zone includes facing the humility of failure. Did you ever meet a child who did not fall off his or her bike while learning how to ride? Seeds of success are within every experience that doesn't work out as planned. Don't allow the occasional stumble or rejection to derail your dreams. Embrace each adversity as one step closer to success. Revise your perspective so that you use failures as a springboard for learning and change. What if failures were something you came to welcome rather than avoid? What if they ultimately empowered you, because you used them as an opportunity for growing in knowledge and wisdom?

Who limits our successes? We do. Pick an area in your life where you've boxed yourself in and challenge yourself to step outside of that box! While you invoke success, build a positive, powerful relationship with failure. Anticipate greater success than ever before, put Peak Life Habits to work, and ascend your personal ladder of joyful greatness. Cut loose and blow the lid off of "almost!"

The entire Habitually Great Methodology is described in detail in *Habitually Great: Master Your Habits, Own Your Destiny.* This book, instead, focuses on those specific Habits that most impact your productivity and time management. Your "Greatness In Action Habit," along with a collection of Right Action Habits are the centerpieces of the forthcoming chapters. By implementing this subset of Peak Life Habits into your daily life with discipline and persistence, you will maximize your efficiency and vanquish any Limiting Habits that have been holding you back. Perfecting your daily schedule, learning how and when to say no, and balancing your many roles, while making the time for and following through on your big dreams and desires, are just some of the skills you will learn in the following pages.

You may be thinking, "I already have a system in place that helps me stay productive." This may be true, and yet chances are there are gems to be found in these pages that you don't know that you don't know. As you read on and work through the exercises ahead, you may also uncover a few Limiting Habits lurking beneath the surface of your conscious awareness that have kept you from reaching your highest aspirations. With all you stand to gain, then, I encourage you to read on and discover how, with several key tweaks and strategic productive enhancements, you can achieve a new level of greatness—greatness, that is, as uniquely defined by you!

PEAK LIFE HABIT SPOTLIGHT:
The "Greatness In Action Habit"

Your **"Greatness In Action Habit"** directs your Actions to fulfill on what you know is right for your heart, and for your life. The life you desire from this point forward, no matter how successful you already are, is the basis for your **"Greatness In Action Habit."**

Greatness, as a concept, is relative. While we can measure the greatness of Olympic athletes, our personal lives require a different yardstick. Greatness for you or your ancestors may have been marked by the courageous and successful act of getting to America, achieving a college or graduate degree, rising to the top of your field, or any number of other personal and community measures, joys, and successes.

Whatever your personal definition of greatness, the **"Greatness In Action Habit"** is your key to mastering Habitually Great Action structures and practices. The "luck" of being in the right place at the right time has little to do with luck. Rather, it is due to consistently taking Action! Hence, the term, "Right Action."

The present moment is all we really have, and your **"Greatness In Action Habit"** is at the core of being fully present in the here and now. The way in which you structure and follow through with the Actions of your life is the chief determining factor in achieving your dreams, intentions, and desires!

The "Greatness In Action Habit" Interrupts:

Avoid Accountability Habit, Overwhelm Habit, Over-Think Habit, Perfectionist Habit, Excuses Habit, I'm Not Worthy Habit

How to read this book:

Habitually Great: Productivity & Time Management is purposefully arranged interactively. There are sixteen chapters, presented in an ascending spiral, with the chapters building upon one another. Within each are a conversation and an interactive exercise for you to put your own pen to paper. These pages present you with a wealth of valuable material, along with new vantage points on the best habitual practices of productivity and time management. When you come upon an exercise, pause and take a few minutes to write your responses, either in the book, where space is provided, or on a separate piece of paper. If you are like me, you won't mind marking up your book—in fact you will enjoy personalizing it with your notations. Others of you like to keep your books crisp and unmarked. Either Habit works! Just be sure to take the time to think through and enjoy writing your responses. This is important for your mind for three key reasons. First, it will help clear out any old Limiting Habit programming. Second, the thinking and writing will immerse you in the practical application of your new Peak Life Habits. Third, and perhaps most importantly, it will help your conscious and subconscious align with your dreams and goals. Let's get started!

CHAPTER 1

INFUSE YOUR LIFE WITH RIGHT ACTION!

"Lots of people know what to do, but few people actually do what they know. Knowing is not enough! You must take action."
—Anthony Robbins

The Nike slogan, "Just Do It," speaks to the success that is within all of our grasps. There is only one problem with taking Nike's advice: the Limiting Habits that stand in our way. When your Limiting Habits threaten your focus, you must do whatever it takes: sidestep them, interrupt them, or create a substitute Habit. Greatness is a commitment and a Habit. Shifting Limiting Habits happens when you understand what you are up against and then declare where you want to go instead, followed by taking positive, preemptive Actions with the discipline and persistence to get you there.

In this chapter, we are going to cover Right Action success structures and Habits that take you beyond "almost." Right Action is positive, disciplined, persistent Action undertaken with clarity, focus, specificity, and measurability. It is the antidote to the poison of Limiting Habits. It reinforces and strengthens our commitment to our desired Outcomes. Right Action is being respectful and appreciative of others and of ourselves. The chart on page 3 shows you several important Right Action Habits (that are a subset of Peak Life Habits) you can adopt as your allies.

When Right Action Habits are in play, despite any of your Limiting Habits that may be lingering around, you are accomplishing things and feeling satisfied. (Keep in mind, Right Action also includes relaxation and nurturing your spiritual, mental, and physical well-being!) Right Action Habits provide the framework for success to walk through your door. They also gather momentum over time and align with circumstances and events around you. The miracles that we perceive—the lucky breaks and "overnight" successes—happen because you are in Right Action. The next time you are in the "right place at the right time" you may recognize that your Right Actions were the most important contributors to getting you there.

TOP 15 RIGHT ACTION HABITS

GREATNESS IN ACTION

- Completion Habit
- Discipline Habit
- Focus & Clarity Habit
- Ground Truth Reality Habit
- Modeling Well Habit
- Pattern Interrupt Habit
- Persistence Habit
- Positive Results Language Habit
- Power Scheduling Habit
- Preemptive Habit
- Proactive Habit
- Right Action Momentum Habit
- Saying No Authentically Habit
- Saying Yes Powerfully Habit
- Teamwork Habit

EXERCISE

Let's dive into our work together by addressing up front the issue of serious "at-stakeness." What do you have "at-stake" in reading this book, working through its exercises, putting its principles into practice, and thereby raising the bar of your own habitual greatness?

Picture in your mind's eye, and use your senses to imagine, see, hear, and feel a handful or more of the dreams and goals you'd like to fulfill in your lifetime, this year, next year, and beyond, whether you've got 10 or 80 years remaining. Just close your eyes for a moment and think of them. Now let's put a little context to them. The little ones, the ones you know you can do on your own—let those be. (You can be sure, though, that this book will help you achieve those faster and easier!) Ah, the big ones: these are the ones that are either true yearnings or proverbial pipe dreams; that challenge you to rise to new heights; that call you forth to do something meaningful and great for yourself or the world; and that you avoid and delay, because you don't even know where or how to start. Let's put those on the table now.

Are you thinking big enough, grand enough, courageous enough? Is there a shortness of breath, a bit of anxiousness in simply thinking about them? Are they so high up or so far off that you can barely feel the early murmur of their heartbeat? What changes must you make, what challenges must you take on, in order to have a truly fulfilled life? It's time to identify and name them. Since we're talking about the majors, here, though, pick just one to three at this point; that is plenty enough of a challenge to get you started.

INFUSE YOUR LIFE WITH RIGHT ACTION!

What's "At-Stake" For Me
Dreams, Intentions, Changes, Contributions,
In This Lifetime

_____
_____
_____
_____
_____

Keep these declarations of "at-stakeness," these great dreams and intentions for your life, in the forefront of your mind as you read and work through the rest of the exercises in this book. If you do, I promise, your life will rise above and beyond "almost" to the place truly called home. Be courageous on the path of habitual greatness!

CHAPTER 2

DRAW INSPIRATION FROM DISCIPLINE

"It is a rough road that leads to the heights of greatness."
—Seneca

As we discussed in the Introduction, success arises out of discipline and persistence, not inspiration. Are you inspired? What if you're not? If you have the "Perfectionist Habit," you just might wait for the perfect type of inspiration before starting anything. For the rest of us, how often have we waited for inspiration to knock us into Right Action? It's tempting to put the inspiration cart before the horse, but too often the results will be disappointing.

Often I'm introduced as a motivational speaker, and the folks in the room excitedly clap as I head for the podium. They're getting ready for a nice dose of inspiration. At least they think they are. The first thing I ask them is, "Hey, how long is a good motivational pep talk going to stay with you once you leave this room?" The answers are always predictable: "An hour ... a few days ... maybe a week." That's not what I'm committed to. If I'm spending my time with you to provide you with the possibility of more joy and success, those timeframes are not sufficient for you to make the Shifts you desire. The insights of motivational talks can give you great feelings. But here's the problem: insights disappear; Habits don't. That's worth repeating:

INSIGHTS DISAPPEAR, HABITS DON'T!

Here's why: insights lead to inspiration, which does not lead to *sustained* Right Action. Now here's the good news: the "Discipline" and "Persistence" Habits do lead to sustained Right Action. Better yet, *discipline leads to inspiration.* That's right. You know that when you have truly applied yourself, whether in school, at sports, at work, or in another venue, success has soon followed. Think back to a time or a success that has felt really good (before your "I'm Not Good Enough Habit," "Confrontation With Success Habit," or other saboteurs jumped in). You were inspired! That inspiration happened *afterward.* Your discipline led to your inspiration, and that's the beauty of the equation. In my motivational talks, we roll up our sleeves, face the ground truth reality of our situations, and get to the real work—the conversations under the conversation, i.e., Habits.

Here's a compelling life example:

DRAW INSPIRATION FROM DISCIPLINE

John[1] was a divorced father of an estranged teenage daughter and the part owner of a family business mired in debt and ownership disputes with his father. He also weighed 330 pounds. He was so heavy that he avoided industry conferences due to his embarrassment about his weight. His "Victim Habit" ran the show. He felt powerless and unhappy.

Here's what John changed: in twelve months, he lost over 80 pounds, reconciled with his daughter at this important time in her life, and bought out his father. All of those took time, discipline, and persistence. He had to push past the self-sabotage moments when all he wanted to do was throw in the towel. That was perhaps the hardest part for him. Coaching was critical in those moments for John. He created an accountable structure—a success structure—to keep him from folding up the tent and giving up. Discipline and persistence lead us through the maze and under, over, or around all obstacles! In the second year of John's Shift, he focused on his company, building quality and accountability systems with a focus on teamwork, and he received a large multi-year contract from one of the top retailers in the industry. He also purchased a new home, adopted a healthy lifestyle, and patterned himself for sustaining greatness. Today John fully enjoys the happiness that he generated, which inspires him greatly. Notice that the inspiration came after *the discipline. John appreciates his successes, takes nothing for granted, and focuses on continuing improvement.*

There are always peaks to climb. John's next peaks are joining the dating scene, expanding his social life and hobbies, and losing another 50 pounds. He uses Habitually Great coaching as a key part of his accountability and as a structure for establishing and exceeding his goals. Coaching is one

---

1 The examples presented in Habitually Great are of real people, actual issues, and bona fide changes. To protect individual confidentiality, personal details have been altered.

of many types of accountability structures you can create for yourself in your quests. However, this book was written so that you would have access to every tool that I used with John.

Just as you did in Chapter 1, Olympic athletes train with inner visualization techniques. They know that their body will manifest what their internal voice says and their mind pictures. They are not afraid of the spotlight; they embrace it. At the same time, their *discipline*, not the spotlight, defines who they are and where they are going. Discipline is their motivator. Great athletes, just like all successful humans, accept that people are watching them. Regardless of the scrutiny, the accountability that they generate is to themselves first and foremost.

It is the same for you as the CEO of your life. Managing your spotlight, just like for great athletes, involves creating structures of discipline and sticking to them, no matter how you are feeling. There is nothing revolutionary about scheduling, staying in Action, and following through. The power tower of Habitual Greatness is in your Habit Mastery, the process of interrupting what has stopped you in the past and instead getting all the way to the checkered flag of joyful completion and success. That's the breakthrough—keeping on and not stopping, no matter what. That is why great athletes and teams *are* great: because they practice, over and over and over. They practice with purpose and intention. They pre-emptively work on circumventing anything that could get in the way, like Limiting Habits. Then they practice some more. Those practices and drills are all scheduled; there's nothing random about their days.

It is the same with first-rate CEOs, great parents, and virtually all people who challenge themselves in their roles to truly be the best they can be: they continue to learn and grow, constantly training and retraining themselves. Right

Action is the ultimate remedy, the preemptive cure for disappointment and the formula for a grand and fulfilled life. It's not about buying lottery tickets; it's about taking sustained Right Action. Discipline and persistence pave the way to *Positively Inspiring Success*! You decide what your trophy case will display and what is important for you to master and feel joyful about.

Discipline and persistence often have to face down a saboteur along the way, though. It's a Limiting Habit that I have often seen challenge sustained greatness: the "Every Other Monther Habit." I've seen this Habit in the behavior of sales persons who consistently over perform and then underperform, in relationships when things are getting too good, and in many situations when the spotlight of success creates areas of paralysis in companies and individuals. It can be every other month, day, or even hour. With Right Action success structures and Habits, though, anyone who has experienced this Habit can overcome it!

LIMITING HABIT SPOTLIGHT: THE "EVERY OTHER MONTHER HABIT"

There are people you observe and admire who are habitually successful. They say, "Thank you," to the spotlights of visibility that naturally accompany their success. The adulation and acknowledgment inspires them to continue with their greatness. They may have the powerful Habits that generate this level of consistent accomplishment such as the *"Believe In Myself Habit"* and *"Greatness Habit."*

For others, in the midst of the success spotlight all of a sudden the "Avoid Accountability Habit" pops up like a jack-in-the-box. We get queasy and uncomfortable with being noticed. We'll under-perform until the spotlight is off of us, and then we'll perform well again. And it happens just as soon as people don't have the expectation of us, so we have that freedom to be great again because no one is watching. Then the cycle continues because we are recognized, and then we panic, under perform, etc. You have likely seen this Habit with promising athletes, spouses, children, and maybe even yourself.

Welcome to the "Every Other Monther Habit." The root of this Habit is about being accountable for success. We all like to succeed, yet paradoxically many of us don't want to be held accountable for maintaining that success. We actually sabotage our performance so that the expectation is diminished. Often this sabotage is at the subconscious level based on the stranglehold of Limiting Habits such as the "Fear Of Success Habit," "I'm Not Good Enough Habit," and "Avoid Accountability Habit." Other Limiting Habits join the chorus too.

The "Every Other Monther Habit" directly correlates to Marianne Williamson's words that: "Your playing small does not serve the world. There is nothing enlightened about shrinking..." Yet shrink we do. Instead, we have to develop that muscle and diminish those Limiting Habits, calling forth powerful Pattern Interrupts and substituting Peak Life Habits, learning that the light is nothing to be afraid of and is something to be consistently humble and proud of. Become Habitually Great at playing in the light!

PATTERN INTERRUPT PEAK LIFE HABITS:

Believe In Myself Habit, Playing Big Habit, Detachment Habit, Greatness Habit, I'm Worthy Habit

DRAW INSPIRATION FROM DISCIPLINE

There is no magic spell for greatness. What we have is something far more reliable—our discipline and persistence, our ever-growing Habit Mastery, and the real-world tools in this book that will keep you in Right Action. The key to Right Action lies in melding your power as the master of your Habits with productivity structures that facilitate your greatness. Are you ready to roll up your sleeves and pave your own road to *Positively Inspiring Success*? If you said yes—or even just maybe—then let's just do it! Let's take some more Right Action steps with this next exercise.

EXERCISE

Defining and managing yourself as a symbol of integrity and purpose is all about knowing who you are as a person, choosing and learning from role models who share your values, and expressing those values through your life and work. Begin that process by identifying and reflecting on your top five core values. Your values are the principles and standards by which you live and work—such as honesty, integrity, peak performance, excellent service, love, creativity, balance, and even fun and adventure. List your core values here in priority order.

1. _____
2. _____
3. _____
4. _____
5. _____

Now think about whom you would like to associate with in the future. These are role models who share your core values and people you would like to have as mentors and peers. List a few of them here, along with your reasons for including them.

ROLE MODEL #1: _____
Reasons: _____
_____
_____

DRAW INSPIRATION FROM DISCIPLINE

ROLE MODEL #2: _____
Reasons: _____
_____
_____

ROLE MODEL #3: _____
Reasons: _____
_____
_____

Next, identify the top three goals you intend to achieve as a result of defining and managing yourself as this symbol of integrity and purpose:

Goal #1: _____
Goal #2: _____
Goal #3: _____

Now consider the success factors. What will help you determine that you have successfully achieved these goals? How will you measure your success?

Success Factor #1: _____
Success Factor #2: _____
Success Factor #3: _____

HABITUALLY GREAT PRODUCTIVITY & TIME MANAGEMENT

To reinforce your thoughts and mental imaging, explain why these success factors are accurate measurements that signify the achievement of your goals:

_____
_____
_____

If you have any concerns about your ability to achieve your goals, what Limiting Habits do you suspect could covertly or overtly threaten your progress? Pick out a few of the top culprits from the **Limiting Habits** appendix (on page 140-141), or if you're aware of some other saboteurs, give them your personalized label or name below.

- _____
- _____
- _____

Your honesty here is a great help! Take heart, though: you also have Habits that will be of great assistance in overcoming obstacles, circumventing any Limiting Habit would-be saboteurs, and realizing your highest aims. List the **Peak Life Habits** (from pages 136-138) you will enlist to help the most.

- _____
- _____
- _____

DRAW INSPIRATION FROM DISCIPLINE

Finally, get ready to head into Action! While you shape your public presence as a symbol of integrity and purpose, what are the key Actions you will take?

ACTION #1: _____

___ I have scheduled to take this Action on/by: _____

___ I have allocated (duration): _____

___ I fulfilled on this Action on: _____

ACTION #2: _____

___ I have scheduled to take this Action on/by: _____

___ I have allocated (duration): _____

___ I fulfilled on this Action on: _____

ACTION #3: _____

___ I have scheduled to take this Action on/by: _____

___ I have allocated (duration): _____

___ I fulfilled on this Action on: _____

There may be more (perhaps many more) than three Actions to fulfill the goals you have declared here. Take these practices into your real world, turn book smarts into street smarts, and expand the Actions that you've launched.

CHAPTER 3

PUT THE "RIGHT ACTION MOMENTUM HABIT" INTO PLAY

"The beginning of a habit is like an invisible thread, but every time we repeat the act we strengthen the strand, add to it another filament, until it becomes a great cable and bind us irrevocably, thought and act."

—Orison Swett Marden

The "Right Action Momentum Habit" works hand in hand with your "Discipline Habit" in leading you to enduring happiness and success. Imagine that you developed the desire and took on the accountability to start something from nothing. For example, envision yourself deciding to do 15 minutes on the stationary bike every day when you are seriously overweight and have not exercised for many years. Sound daunting?

In fact, most great achievements begin as mere ideas with no muscle mass to support them. With the initial push and continuing discipline that come from putting the "Right Action Momentum Habit" into play in your life, though, your intentions gain mass and momentum, grow, develop, and ascend.

The key is to engage your "Discipline Habit," schedule your Actions, and keep pushing forward, inch by inch, step by step. It may involve a lot of sweat equity, as if you're trying to push a boulder that just refuses to budge, yet you keep pushing. So there may be some hardship, a bit of struggle, sweat, rigor, and then step by step, day by day, with a setback here and there, as you keep it all going, finally a tipping point is reached. Interestingly, that tipping point may go unnoticed, because you are so focused on staying with the rhythm, building momentum, and recovering any missteps. As the weeks go by, all of a sudden you find yourself riding 45 minutes at a clip, easy as pie.

The "Right Action Momentum Habit" is a positive, intentional, step-by-step momentum builder that leads to the positive side of inertia. Like a kid on a swing furiously pumping his legs hoping to soar, your dream may not pick up much momentum at first. Luckily, your "Discipline Habit" keeps you from giving up, and lo and behold, steadily the effort lessens and you're swinging with the treetops, feeling the exhilaration of success. That is how the "Right Action Momentum Habit" works in every arena—be it exercise, weight loss, career ascension, wealth, or general happiness in life.

Through your continuous, determined, and patient application of the Habitually Great methodology, even if you stumble at times, even if the rubber band exerts its backward pull on occasion, your "Right Action Momentum Habit" will help you recover your ground and power forward. It will keep you moving onward and upward on your own unique, inspired path of greatness.

PEAK LIFE HABIT SPOTLIGHT:
The "Right Action Momentum Habit"

The **"Right Action Momentum Habit"** is about traversing step by step toward your greatness, like a glider that soars over extraordinary terrain and lands in the field of change with grace and integration. It is about simplifying and taking small bites while not allowing ourselves to be overwhelmed by the large and important goals we have targeted. With this Peak Life Habit we place our "Self-Sabotage Habit" to the sideline while we act as our own mother ship, pulling ourselves to the tipping point of bright blue skies where our momentum is established and we are self-propelling with inspired confidence, soaring on our own.

It is exactly the opposite of the "Doom Loop Habit," which is all about optimistically expecting miracles to happen overnight and being disappointed and stressed when our immediate, frantic efforts don't pay off.

When we are exercising our **"Right Action Momentum Habit"** we are staying in Action, interrupting and side-stepping Limiting Habits, keeping our forward motion and achieving our goals. This is one of the most important Peak Life Habits. It will enable you to remain steadfastly in Right Action, ascending the important areas of your life, powerful and focused in your own right.

The "Right Action Momentum Habit" Interrupts:

Avoid Accountability Habit, Confrontation With Success Habit, Doom Loop Habit, Waiting For The Shoe To Drop Habit, Paralysis Habit

A simple example of the "Right Action Momentum Habit" involved the following breakthrough for one of our coaching clients:

Chloe is a Director at a large accounting firm and spent her days reading tax returns, reading tax research, reading emails, meeting with clients, etc. When she got home at night, she also had roles as wife, mother, homework assistant, and Girl Scout Troup leader. She loved to read non-fiction yet had not read a book in a few years, feeling that there simply wasn't enough spare time. (She had developed a "Victim Habit" in her relationship with time.) She had a desire to be learning about all sorts of other subjects, feeding her starved curiosity. How could she develop a success structure around reading with so many roles to which she allocated time?

With her Habitually Great coach, she analyzed her time and roles, and she decided to implement something simple: a "Right Action Momentum Habit." She scheduled 15 minutes each night for reading. It didn't sound like much at first, and she was interested to see if it would have any impact. To accomplish her goal, there was a Limiting Habit that had to be changed first: her "Perfectionist Habit" from which, over the years, she'd come to believe that she must have at least an hour or more to immerse herself in a good book, and she liked to finish any chapter she started in the same sitting. Well, 15 minutes a night was not going to take her from chapter to chapter. It was time to change her perspective and make her expectations of herself, given her current circumstances, more reasonable.

So she started, just 15 minutes a night, and found it fulfilling—and liberating, too, not to have to read a whole chapter. It was even more fun to discover just how much she was in fact reading each week and how much she was enjoying it. The steady commitment to her reading list kept the material

PUT THE "RIGHT ACTION MOMENTUM HABIT" INTO PLAY

fresh and easier to retain from night to night. Within the first three weeks, with her steady "Right Action Momentum Habit," she had finished a book that she had wanted to read for three years.

Reading is a simple example and, for Chloe, an important one. With a little introspection, you may find you have one or more clear-cut challenges of your own—even if they seem like minor ones—that you can face, turn into goals, and develop reasonable success structures to support you in realizing those aims. Start today by identifying one of those goals and setting up a realistic success structure—one that only requires you to take small, eminently doable Action steps—to reach it. Then, no matter what, follow through, maintain your commitment and momentum, so you can find yourself just as surprised and delighted as Chloe by both the process and the fulfillment, resolution, or completion of your issue or goal.

HABITUALLY GREAT PRODUCTIVITY & TIME MANAGEMENT

> **PEAK LIFE HABIT SPOTLIGHT:**
> **The "Success Structures Habit"**
>
> Encourage your *Habitually Great* productivity and time management practices with the support of your **"Success Structures Habit."** With this Habit, you adopt, implement, sustain, and enhance structures that keep you taking Right Action, sustaining and building upon your inspired path of greatness. Some of those success structures are:
>
> - Schedule Yourself Powerfully
> - Employ One Simple Daily To-Do System
> - Banish Distractions
> - Carve Out Solitary Work Blocks
> - Nail Down Your Stop Doing List
> - Commit To Your Start Doing List
> - Practice Reverse Timeline Scheduling
> - Master the Art of Delegation
>
> As the wheel of your **"Success Structures Habit"** begins to roll forward, recognize Limiting Habits that get in the way, and shift to Peak Life Habits.
>
> **The "Success Structures Habit" Interrupts:**
>
> *Procrastination Habit, Someday/One Day Habit, Fear of Success Habit, Backsliding Habit, Can't Say No Habit, Regret Habit, Almost Habit*

This is how Right Action works. Welcome to greatness! In case you are wondering, I am not over-simplifying the path to success. There is no single tipping point, no celebrity TV host or Fortune 100 CEO that saves your day, no point when somebody pulls a lever and turns on all the lights in the house, and then thousands of your favorite people stand to applaud. Instead, the people and companies that succeed are the ones that focus steadily, without fanfare, and stay on the path toward reaching their clearly articulated, specific, and measurable goals and intentions.

PUT THE "RIGHT ACTION MOMENTUM HABIT" INTO PLAY

Exercise

Identify an area of your life you would like to improve, as well as a specific, measurable goal for improvement you are committed to achieving.

Area: _____

Measurable Goal: _____

Using these questions as a guide, assess your current level of discipline in this area:

How committed am I really to being the best I can be, to having what I say I want to have, and to doing what I say I will in this area? Why? _____

_____

_____

What obstacles have I allowed to slow my progress in the past in this area? Why? _____

_____

How do I plan to overcome these obstacles and brush aside any distractions or interruptions to my plan? _____

_____

_____

HABITUALLY GREAT PRODUCTIVITY & TIME MANAGEMENT

Now identify a few specific and measurable Actions you will take and accountability structures you will use to build Right Action Momentum on the road to achieving your goal. Then describe the level of focus, discipline, and rigor that may be required to complete each Action. As you complete each Action step, return here to note the date. And be sure to take a moment to appreciate your efforts. Celebrate!

ACTION #1: _____

    I have scheduled to take this Action on/by:_____

    I have allocated (duration): _____

    Accountability Structure:_____

    Focus/discipline/rigor required: _____

    I fulfilled on this Action on: _____

ACTION #2: _____

    I have scheduled to take this Action on/by:_____

    I have allocated (duration): _____

    Accountability Structure:_____

    Focus/discipline/rigor required: _____

    I fulfilled on this Action on: _____

ACTION #3: _____

    I have scheduled to take this Action on/by:_____

    I have allocated (duration): _____

    Accountability Structure:_____

    Focus/discipline/rigor required: _____

    I fulfilled on this Action on: _____

PUT THE "RIGHT ACTION MOMENTUM HABIT" INTO PLAY

Finally, considering the Actions you've scheduled, can you identify which Limiting Habits might challenge your building Right Action Momentum and maintaining discipline on the road to your goal? For each of these potential saboteurs, choose a Peak Life Habit to which you will commit to Shifting for optimal results. The chart you will find in Appendix C on pages 142-146 can help you identify your Shifts.

Limiting Habits you Shift to Peak Life Habits:

Limiting Habit #1: _____
       Shifts to Peak Life Habit: _____

Limiting Habit #2: _____
       Shifts to Peak Life Habit: _____

Limiting Habit #3: _____
       Shifts to Peak Life Habit: _____

CHAPTER 4

GET CLEAR ON YOUR MULTIPLE ROLES IN LIFE

> *"All the world's a stage, and all the men and women merely players: they have their exits and their entrances, and one man in his time plays many parts..."*
>
> —Shakespeare

Let's deepen our analysis of time in your life by looking at the key roles you play in those areas where you invest a substantial amount time on a regular basis. For starters, you may have a role as a partner/spouse, boyfriend/girlfriend, parent, son/daughter, extended family member, caregiver, pet owner, cook, shopper, carpooler, commuter, or school board member. You probably also, of course, play one or more roles in your career and industry. And you may have still more in the areas of managing your health and fitness, spirituality, hobbies, and community. Note there is also your individual role of "rest recharger." That role is one of the most important. (Consider, for instance, that at least 25% or more of your time is allocated to sleep.) You must manage that role well so you have enough energy and, ideally, vitality to direct toward all of your many commitments. In our busy lives, regardless of age or status, the list of our roles has become quite extensive, perhaps too much so.

Most of us have at least five or more basic areas with roles that are best served by scheduling appropriate time for them. We have work, relationships, fitness, family, spiritual/religious practices, finances, and hobbies. Notice that as you look at any single category, you are likely to see that you have multiple roles within each category. When you add to that number all of your other roles, there is a lot of organizing and scheduling to do. Roles are areas of commitment and accountability, and most of us underestimate what we are accountable for and what others expect from us, as well as what we expect from ourselves. When the rubber meets the road, we often find we are behind and overwhelmed by the myriad of demands of our roles.

You may be thinking there are roles and areas in your life into which you want to invest more time, and wondering, "Where is that time going to come from?" If you don't schedule most of these areas, the greatness that you desire may never occur. Your relationships may only be so good; you may only get to enjoy your hobbies just so much. Perhaps you've always wanted to write a book, for example, yet have never scheduled much less followed through on the time to do it. A quick look at your myriad roles might explain why the time hasn't been allocated. Add a dollop of Limiting Habits into the mix, and that book isn't likely to reach the printing press. Sound familiar? It does to your humble author too.

EXERCISE

Take a moment to reflect on a few areas of commitment and responsibility in which you'd like to really step it up. Here, we'll sketch a brief portrait of these areas: we'll name them, identify your unique roles within them, and then set specific goals for each of these related roles. You will want to select an immediate goal (achievable within the next few weeks or months), a short-term goal (within six months), and also a long-term goal. And if you like the results, later, you can work up portraits of every key area of your life and set specific goals for all of your roles.

Life Area #1: _____

Role: _____

Average time spent weekly: _____

Overall Theme/Intention For This Role: _____

_____

Immediate goal: _____

Short-term goal: _____

Long-term goal: _____

Life Area #2: _____

Role: _____

Average time spent weekly: _____

Overall Theme/Intention For This Role: _____

_____

Immediate goal: _____
Short-term goal: _____
Long-term goal: _____

Life Area #3: _____
Role: _____
Average time spent weekly: _____
Overall Theme/Intention For This Role: _____
_____
Immediate goal: _____
Short-term goal: _____
Long-term goal: _____

Remember: the abundance of a life well lived and savored includes committing to and scheduling for the roles that are most important. You will enjoy the satisfaction of knowing that you are investing your time in what *you* decide matters.

CHAPTER 5

APPRECIATE THAT TIME IS JUST TIME

> *"Dost thou love life? Then do not squander time, for that the stuff life is made of."*
> —Benjamin Franklin

All right, fess up. Let's tackle the issue of time with good old-fashioned honesty. How often have you justified something not happening or felt distressed about an intention you didn't realize or a goal you didn't complete—or even make a good start toward—due to time constraints?

A key corollary of the principle of Right Action for Habitual Greatness is to keep an eye on the clock. The time issue often comes up in our conversations with statements like: "There is not enough time," "I have no time," "I need more hours in the day," "I'd like to buy some time," and "What happened to the time?" What are some of your habitual Beliefs and internal and external pet phrases about time?

Our thoughts and comments about time are often a covert displacement of what we are actually refusing to deal with. We play the time card instead of looking directly at our Limiting Habits to see what really puts up the roadblock. When your time conversation comes up, ask yourself, "What is this conversation displacing?" Is it a covert excuse for your "Confrontation With Success Habit?" Is it a cover-up for an "I'm Not Good Enough Habit?" There are certainly many demands today on our time. Unfortunately, this state of affairs gives us many more excuses to hide behind a limiting conversation about time. Down the road, you'll be summoning your "Regret Habit" and ruminating about how you could have "made the time."

Here's an alternative: deal with it! Identify what you are really refusing to deal with when you put your "overwhelmed with not enough time" conversation into the forefront of your thoughts. Time is just time. Say it again, louder: "Time is just time!" It is "time" to alter your relationship to and prioritize your time in a manner that supports your relationships, joys, and goals. In the pages immediately ahead are plenty more Right Action structures and Peak Life Habits that will assist you.

The good news is that time is not in exceedingly short supply. In fact, it's one of the great equalizers. There are 24 hours in a day, 60 minutes in an hour, 60 seconds in a minute—for everyone, no matter how privileged or disenfranchised. There is neither more nor less, and there never will be. We have the privilege of being able to allocate that time to our roles and priorities. Acknowledging this truth allows us to be authentic about what we can and cannot accomplish. You can alter your relationship to time by prioritizing what is important and being responsible about how you allocate your days, hours, and minutes. Immediately and for the long term, institute the practice of the "Saying No Authentically Habit" combined with the "Saying Yes Powerfully Habit." Both will go a long way toward taking control of how your time is allocated. I guarantee a Shift toward greatness will happen!

EXERCISE

How would you characterize your Time Habits in relation to deadlines and appointments?

_____
_____
_____

What are your favorite expressions about time or the perceived lack thereof?

- _____
- _____
- _____

What are your other Habits about time?

- _____
- _____
- _____

What Beliefs do you have about your Time Habits?

- _____
- _____
- _____

APPRECIATE THAT TIME IS JUST TIME

What are your Beliefs, more generally, about time? For example, do you feel that there's never enough time? Do you feel that time is just time?

- _____
- _____
- _____

How would you characterize the Time Habits of some of your family members, friends, colleagues, or customers in relation to deadlines and appointments?

PERSON #1: _____
Time Habits: _____
_____
_____

PERSON #2: _____
Time Habits: _____
_____
_____

PERSON #3: _____
Time Habits: _____
_____
_____

What do you think about people in general with various types of Time Habits?

I think early people are: _____

_____

I think on-time people are: _____

_____

I think late people are: _____

_____

I think people who vary their Time Habits are: _____

_____

And what do you think they truly think about themselves?

Early people think they are: _____

_____

On-time people think they are: _____

_____

Late people think they are: _____

_____

People who vary their Time Habits think they are: _____

_____

APPRECIATE THAT TIME IS JUST TIME

Keep in mind: love, compassion, kindness, and detachment will always help you power through difficult moments. So, if you catch yourself thinking of chronically late people as being rude, selfish, and disorganized, take a step back and cast a compassionate eye on their situation. They're not trying to offend you. In fact, their behavior is probably not about you at all. (Sorry.) More likely, they see themselves as overwhelmed, having too many things to do and lacking sufficient time to do them. Similarly, if you feel irked by consistently early people and find yourself thinking of them as being pushy or needing to get a life, stop a minute. Recognize that they probably maintain this Habit, instead, to show respect and consideration for your time. How wonderful!

Be compassionate and kind toward others, no matter what Habits are running them. Fully accept all the people you know, live, and work worth. And love them exactly the way they are—and exactly the way they aren't! Or choose kindly not to interact with them. It is that simple. Don't expect anyone else to change. The only person you have the power to change in your life is *you*.

CHAPTER 6

FILL YOUR BUCKETS OF TIME WITH PURE GOLD

"There is never enough time to do everything, but there is always enough time to do the most important thing."

—Brian Tracy

Doing a "Buckets of Time" analysis of your life gives you the nitty-gritty understanding of how you spend your days and hours—and may waste much of them without realizing the allocation or cost. You can see how much time you are parked, with the time meter ticking, in each Bucket. Through this simple analytical tool, you can clarify what changes you want to make, as well as how you will make those changes by investing your time in a manner consistent with the Right Actions and accountabilities toward your goals and dreams. You will be able to see how your time is allocated within any particular role. You may also want to pause and look deeper under the hood, to illuminate roles with important responsibilities you may not even have realized existed for you, yet are time consumers too.

The reality check your Buckets of Time analysis provides may confirm that you have been attempting magic tricks with time. Let's save magic for the magicians and get grounded in reality. As you review and reflect upon your analysis, it will become clear to you where to make changes in your schedule and in each of your roles.

PEAK LIFE HABIT SPOTLIGHT:
The "Ground Truth Reality Habit"

The Habitually Great program is a ground truth reality check about what your Habits (and you) have been up to. Are you really aligned with your goals and desires? Are you really happy? What is in the way? When you peel back your public image, what are the real truths about your station in life? This is the contrast between the Limiting "Official Truth Habit" and the Peak Life *"Ground Truth Reality Habit."*

The "Official Truth Habit" is the façade that you often may live in. Are you putting a positive spin on things to avoid confronting the brutal facts? Are you an optimist with a "Fantasy Habit," pretending that your life is different than it is, avoiding making changes because a Limiting Habit about worthiness, effort or fear is holding you back?

At work are you courageous enough to manage people with accountability or do you choose artificial harmony over productive conflict? Have you been more concerned about popularity than accountability? Your "Official Truth Habit" has kept you paralyzed long enough. It is time to be accountable for seeing the ground truth and taking Action that aligns with your reality.

Additionally, when you apply your *"Ground Truth Reality Habit"* to your Language Habits, you may also see what you have been "trying" or "needing" to do for a long time. If you have been "trying" to do something for three years, the ground truth may be that you are never going to do it.

Look reality straight in the eye, stop dancing around it, and stop making compromises with your integrity. Root out the Limiting Habits that get in the way of your *"Ground Truth Reality Habit."* What are they? Be accountable for being brave, bold and authentic, for seeing the truth in the status of your well being, place and purpose, career and relationships, and be responsible for creating what you truly want, starting right now. Follow the prescription for Right Action with unwavering resolve. Bring some supporting Peak Life Habits along for your *"Ground Truth Reality Habit,"* including the *"Proactive Habit," "Courage Habit,"* and *"Playing Big Habit."*

The "Ground Truth Reality Habit" Interrupts:

Artificial Harmony Habit, Fantasy Habit, Optimist Habit, Why Bother Habit, Looking Good Habit, Procrastination Habit

So let's get started with an easy and persuasive application of this approach. (You can find a more in-depth analysis tool for multiple roles in the *Habitually Great Workbooks* available at www.habituallygreat.com.) Choose one of the roles you identified in Chapter 4. Determine the specific activities required to fulfill that role, and note the number of hours you are currently allocating for each activity. If your analysis shows that the goals and activities you set for that role aren't currently supported by your Buckets of Time allocation, that contradiction must be corrected! Note the number of hours you would ideally prefer to allocate for each activity, and the number you believe you could realistically allocate in the future.

The key is to use this exercise as a tool, analyzing your roles and goals one at a time. We allocate our time in so many areas that it is crucial to see where exactly it is consumed. Given this full breadth of information, you many find it's also high time to look at Limiting Habits like the "Do It Myself" and "Can't Say No" Habits. What are you going to delegate or ask someone else to do? How are you going to achieve a balanced, awesome life with all the stuff you have on your plate already? The first step to answering these sorts of questions is running a good, honest "Buckets of Time" investigation.

EXERCISE

Role: _____

Average time spent weekly in this role: _____

Immediate goal: _____

Short-term goal: _____

Long-term goal: _____

Specific Role Activity	Current Number of Hours Weekly	Ideal Number of Hours Weekly	Realistic Number of Hours Weekly	Time of Day/ Day of Week
TOTALS				

HABITUALLY GREAT PRODUCTIVITY & TIME MANAGEMENT

Changes To Be Made: _____
_____
_____

Effect on immediate goal: _____
_____

Effect on short-term goal: _____
_____

Effect on long-term goal: _____
_____

Note: If you're noticing a "Resignation" or "Skepticism" Habit popping up about now, STOP! Step out of your box, identify what additional Limiting Habits may be stopping you from taking Right Action, and then rework the box until you make a breakthrough. Do not allow an internal voice to talk you out of this. Just consider it a clue that there is an old self-defeating conversation under the conversation here—i.e., a Limiting Habit—and Shift back toward being Habitually Great!

CHAPTER 7

SCHEDULE YOURSELF FOR HABITUAL GREATNESS

"Nothing can add more power to your life than concentrating all of your energies on a limited set of targets."
—Nido Qubein

I remember a time many years ago when I did not keep a schedule. Yet I was always scheduled; I just didn't have it written anywhere. I was proud of the fact that I kept everything in my head and could always remember my schedule for the upcoming days and weeks. That was a lot of mental real estate occupied with scheduling. I didn't realize that the head gymnastics I was doing with my schedule were taking away from my capacity to be fully present in the moment. Today, after many years as a student of productivity and time management, I can see how much more in-the-moment freedom and brain power I have at the table, so to speak. I carefully capture the commitments, to-do's, and details of my upcoming days and weeks, using a shareable calendar tool. I actually don't know what I'm doing tomorrow and never worry about it, because it is all written, organized, and planned! When you blend Peak Life Habits with Power Scheduling, you will bring all of your desires into reality with ease and brilliance. You will become comfortable starting *and* finishing anything you commit to.

If you have already achieved mastery with creating your schedule, you know that the structure of a schedule gives you the accountability, perseverance, and continuity to keep on going. See what tips you may find in the following pages, even with your highly effective scheduling protocols. Mastering a new level of attention to scheduling is often the missing link to productively staying organized and in Action and achieving habitually great results, no matter how much there is to do.

If you prefer not to keep a formal schedule, be aware of pitfalls you may not have anticipated. We sometimes mistakenly feel that not having a schedule provides us with the ability to be free, flexible, and spontaneous, when, in reality, that "freedom" is an empty void that doesn't get us anywhere worth going. Without a schedule we have no accountability to actually do or accomplish anything.

At every Habitually Great keynote speech, workshop, or seminar, there are always war stories from the planner. I'm amazed by the methods of madness involving schedules. Our education system neglects to teach us about a few key areas of life. How many of us have had training in Leadership, Relationships, Financial Management, Fitness, Nutrition, and Time Management? Whether you are the crackerjack of scheduling or less proficient with your calendar than you want to be, here are two real life stories that may make you smile.

SCHEDULE YOURSELF FOR HABITUAL GREATNESS

Karen came to me after years of crippling her output in the name of spontaneity. She told herself that structuring her schedule would be too limiting, so she kept it all in her head. She knew exactly what day and time every appointment was, and she planned her days and weeks with her internal Memory Planner. She shunned watches—and always knew what time it was, too. She could remember phone numbers, dates—everything—and rarely missed a beat.

And therein lay the problem: her practice of keeping track of time and schedules in her Memory Planner left her mind so full that there was little room left for creative juices to flow. All the effort she was putting into avoiding the perceived limitations of a schedule was in fact limiting her productivity. Her devotion to her old story about her spontaneous schedule actually left her with few accomplishments and little freedom.

Today she is amazed at what she accomplishes. She uses a cloud-based calendar, has a perfect to-do system and has established structures and Right Action Habits that have her producing remarkable results every day.

Karen's breakthrough was in the discovery that with a rigorous "Power Scheduling Habit" her head is clear to focus in the moment, because her schedule manages her life. With that freedom, she noticed a remarkable expansion in her ability to be fully present, and that provides for real spontaneity. Plus, she now has more free time than ever to do many more things that she loves because she schedules the time for them!

Take a look at your Habits concerning scheduling and spontaneity. If it is independence you want, you can create it by depending on one straightforward system and thereby freeing up the rest of your mind. If you are concerned and are equating a structured scheduling paradigm with lost spontaneity, then create a Habit of scheduling a few hours into each day where you have nothing scheduled except spontaneity. You will likely be more spontaneous than ever, because you have allocated the time to be so.

Jeff is a father, husband, heart patient, and the General Manager for a large company. In the midst of a Habitually Great seminar with his key executives and managers, he revealed that he kept one schedule on his office computer, a second on his refrigerator, a third in his car, and yet another for his personal life that he carried around with him. His fear and resistance to having one central schedule stemmed from the turmoil that had ensued a few years ago when he lost the one schedule and contact database he was keeping at the time. This event left him blanketed by a fear of losing everything again if he maintained a single planning system.

In the grips of this new Belief, he created new Actions and a new Habit with the Outcome of having several schedules scattered about. In spite of his commitment to being exceptional in all of his roles, his new scheduling Habit was setting him up to underperform and disappoint everyone. He tried to cross-coordinate the various schedules every day, even though it became increasingly impossible to do so. As a case in point, he told us about a single afternoon a few weeks earlier on which he had made it to a late-afternoon doctor's appointment noted on his personal schedule yet missed both his sons' soccer games (written months ago on the refrigerator calendar) and a brief sit-down with a job applicant (which one of his managers had set up with a secretary to whom he had mentioned neither the medical appointment nor the game).

His productivity was suffering because his (now subconscious) fear of losing his schedule was controlling his life.

The structure of a Habitually Great Power Schedule gives you a home for the desires and goals in your mind and heart, translating them into accountable Action steps and milestones. Be gentle, yet disciplined, with yourself as you ramp up your scheduling and follow-through Habits. Well-designed schedules and accountability to the Actions declared within them carry you forth to where you want to be.

> **BENEFITS OF HABITUALLY GREAT POWER SCHEDULING**
>
> - *Organizing All Areas:* Work, Fitness, Relationships, Family, Goals
> - *Fulfilling:* Your roles and your desires, dreams and goals
> - *Transcending:* Large tasks by cutting them into small pieces
> - *Keeping:* Your word – fulfill your commitments
> - *Being Responsible:* For your "On Time Habit"
> - *Practicing:* Reverse Timeline Scheduling
> - *Notating:* Desired Outcomes & To-Do's
> - *Rescheduling:* Strengthen your integrity
> - *Completing:* Everything you touch
> - *Automating:* Everything you can
> - *Saying:* No and meaning no

Habitually Great Power Scheduling begins by putting everything that is important to you in your schedule—including to-do's, "Honey"-do's, workouts, hobbies, and the rest of it. By keeping track of your life in one universal place, nothing falls through the cracks. The particular type of schedule that works best is up to you. Most of us already have cloud-based, computer, mobile, or paper-based planners. All types work well, as long as you pick just one. The single most important change you can make in your life is to schedule it effectively, keep to your word, and keep your schedule. As you implement or enhance your universal schedule, here are some worthwhile considerations.

Empower Your Schedule

Some us often have such a strong "Avoid Authority Habit" that we tend to avoid our schedule because it's telling us what to do. We don't like being told what to do, and yet somehow this inanimate object becomes a feared or despised authority figure. Get over this one! As we take on being masters in time management, scheduling, and staying in Right Action, we may occasionally sabotage our schedule with this old Habit. In those moments, pause, take a deep breath, and then get right back into power by saying, "I love my schedule. I created it to assist me with my happiness. It's just part of me, not a separate entity!"

Notate Desired Outcomes

Begin the practice of writing the Outcomes you desire along with your scheduled items. Many people love this practice once they start it. They feel a stronger sense of accomplishment and intention. For example, instead of writing: "5:00 P.M. strategy meeting with Diane," perhaps write "Upbeat meeting with Diane where we argue/cajole and create a great strategy to align on." Notating your desired Outcomes is good practice for your "Believe in Myself Habit" and your "Determined to Succeed Habit." You have the direct power to create what you imagine!

Create an Interruptions/Distractions Floater

Here is an excellent tool for taking over the interruptions and curtailing the distractions in your day. Compile a list on a pad for a day or two of all of your interruptions and distractions while also jotting down the approximate time that is consumed. For example:

<u>Stopped to watch the news this morning–10 min.</u>
<u>Unplanned errand–35 min.</u>
<u>Stopped work & read a magazine article at my desk–15 min.</u>
<u>John came into my office to discuss personal problems–20 min.</u>
<u>Phone/text with Mom, spouse, and two friends while at work–25 min.</u>

That's an hour and 45 minutes, right there! When you start to see how much time you are expending for the "unplanned," you may be surprised. Scheduling well requires applying the principles of your "Ground Truth Reality Habit." Identify how much time in the day, on average, you are interrupted or otherwise distracted. If this calculates to an hour or two per day, start scheduling the time to cover those interruptions. This is what I call the "floater." Generally we don't know exactly when those moments will occur; we just know that they will at some point during the day. So make sure that if the predictable amount of time for the daily *unexpected* is typically an hour and a half, you have blocked off a total of 90 minutes per day in your planner.

You must schedule for this "floater" of time or else these distractions and interruptions will consume the time you've already set for other top-priority Actions. If you don't account for these, you may notice that you are perpetually driven by your "Overwhelm" and "Distress" Habits.

Here's how you schedule this floater: take any block or blocks of time you choose and mark them as your "Interruptions Floater." For example, you may choose to rope off 1:00 P.M. to 2:30 P.M. Monday through Friday at the office, or you could schedule three 30-minute segments throughout the day every day. Pick any variety of time blocks summing to 90 minutes you like, just do it!

Creating a floater of real time prepares you for the inevitable daily interruptions. Perhaps interruptions are even part of your job description. I chuckled when I observed a client cursing the phone every time it rang. The calls were from his customers, and if the phone didn't ring, he'd be out of a job! Together we worked to give him a new approach to and appreciation for those calls—by having him schedule a two-hour floater every day to accommodate the reality that those calls would occur and were an integral part of his job.

Here's the secret to the "floater:" you allocate bona fide, specific times in the day for it, and it shuffles. You have two choices for how it moves:

One, simply proceed with your day, shuffling your schedule, knowing you have time for everything, and accommodate interruptions when they occur. That's why we call it a floater; interruptions happen randomly during the day, not always "on schedule." As long as you've allocated real time for their occurrence, you simply use a portion of that time when they occur. Your schedule accommodates the time, and the flexible parts of your schedule Shift, such that a report you plan to complete from 2:00 to 3:30 P.M. may have its actual start and stop times adjusted, yet no time is taken away from it. Meanwhile, the hard and fast scheduled meetings, conference calls, doctor's appointments, soccer games, etc. stay right on their timeline.

A second option is to corral your interruptions and distractions into the exact time of the floater you have scheduled. For example, if you have set aside from 10:00 to 11:30 A.M. for unforeseen interruptions, and a client calls unexpectedly (and it's not a crisis), a staff member walks in for a chat, or your best friend calls for what is predictably a 15-minute conversation, what do you do? Simply explain your new system and make a compassionate request to schedule with them for a specific time that is within your scheduled floater for that day. Again, you won't feel stressed, because you've already set aside the necessary amount of time, and colleagues, family, and friends will appreciate that you are allocating real time to them. Both of these methods work well, and the result is that you feel calm and complete at the end of a given day, because you have created a schedule based on reality!

Reschedule and Don't Sweat It

Have you noticed that sometimes you get aggravated if you mess up your schedule—when you didn't do what you said you were going to do, when you forgot to do something, when something got in the way, or when you were interrupted in the middle of something important? Starting now, set any and all negativity aside. What Limiting Habits are you invoking with these negative thoughts? Perhaps your "Hard On Myself Habit" or your "Perfectionist Habit?" How about a simple, humble acknowledgement, instead, an "Oops, I missed that" or "I didn't finish that *today*"? No self-judgment, just the facts.

Instead of suffering over it, reschedule it. Reschedule the meeting, the workout, the piano practice, or that hour to write.

HABITUALLY GREAT PRODUCTIVITY & TIME MANAGEMENT

This is critical; by taking positive, proactive steps, you further ingrain the "Success" and "Feeling Good" Habits. As soon as you stop suffering, trust me, it's going to be a lot easier to reschedule whenever an unexpected situation arises and puts a kink in your schedule—as it inevitably will.

Remember Play Time

It is vital that downtime gets plugged into your schedule. Block out hours to do what you love to do alongside of work and family commitments—social and recreational activities, hobbies, and such. Scheduling play time also means setting aside blocks of time without filling in what the hours are even for—spontaneously *in-the-moment* time. Invoke your "Lightening Up Habit!" You'll decide what to do in those moments. Remember also to block out time for vacation, weeks, months, or even a year or two in advance.

Discover Extra Golden Hours

Consider for a moment, what would life be like if you took one day and charted how you spent its entirety, from start to finish, from head on the pillow to head back on the pillow? You would learn a lot about where all that "lost time" has been hiding. So why not do it now? Take just one day, and sit down with a pad and pen in hand (or, of course, at the computer, if you prefer) to track and log how you spent all your time. If it seems helpful, you might even use five-minute increments, so you capture all the little stuff that adds up so quickly.

To help jog your memory, ask yourself questions like, How long did it take to drive to work? What did I do while at work?

What did I do with the family? Add up all the time for social networking, surfing the web, texting, phone calls, tasks, (bathroom breaks and shower time, too!), commuting, errands, and chores. And don't forget to include the interruptions that pulled you off course for a bit and any distractions you may have caved into frittering away some precious minutes or hours on. Almost all of us will ultimately find at least an hour or two a day of poorly used time. Imagine if we could reclaim that. We could devote those extra golden hours to taking the lid off and propelling smartly toward our goals. Or we could choose something just as important; kicking back and enjoying the sweet feeling of pure relaxation!

An important aspect of Right Action lies in the combined discipline of being a focused and diligent scheduler along with keeping your word and following through on the Actions you have chosen to include in your planner. Therefore, creating a *realistic* schedule is central to achieving your objectives. You will reap major benefits from implementing the above tips, and this next exercise will benefit you even more, plus give you the opportunity to upgrade some of the scheduling fundamentals.

Before we dive into the exercise, though, take a look at the next page for a model of a typical day in a Habitually Great power schedule. In fact, it's a day-in-the-life of your humble author. The example may or may not be relevant to you. Your schedule will reflect your life's own cadence. Hopefully, though, it will provide some food for thought. Notice, for instance, how I've notated my outcomes and included an interruptions floater.

Whether you are young or older, an executive, an entrepreneur, a home-based Mom or Dad with a bunch of kids to shepherd around, or a working single person without even a pet to care for, you have plenty to do. Be sure your passions, desires, and goals inform your schedule, making it a daily, living document of a set of success structures unique to you.

SCHEDULE YOURSELF FOR HABITUAL GREATNESS

SAMPLE SCHEDULE

November 12

Time	Activity	Notes/Added Action Items
6:30a – 8:15a	Wake-up/Picture the day and set positive intentions! 10-minute cardio warm-up. Organize/help around the house, shower/shave/toilet. Make and drink smoothie. Pack tennis bag and drive to work. (Drink water)	
8:15a – 9:00a	Organize files/desk for today. Check and respond to email/vm messages. Reading time (20 mins).	
9:00a – 9:35a	Great phone session with client. (Drink water)	
9:35a – 10:00a	Meet with Julie, review Q1 program schedule, finalize travel arrangement decisions and workshop locations.	
10:00a – 10:30a	Full staff meeting: review workshop handouts, timeline and logistics for today's program.	
10:30a – 11:30a	Great phone session with client. (Drink water)	
11:30a – 12:15p	Floater for interruptions, schedule changes, errands, calls, etc.	
12:15a – 1:00p	Eat a healthy protein/veggie meal at desk, check email/vm.	
1:00p – 1:20p	Drive to conference center, relax, get ready for workshop. (No phone calls)	
1:20p – 1:45p	Check in with staff, final tweaks on room setup.	
1:45p – 3:45p	Deliver fun and focused 2-hour workshop module (this is module 3 or 5), facilitate a good teamwork and accountability shift!	
3:45p – 4:15p	Informal time with participants, quick debrief to thank staff.	
4:15p – 4:45p	Return to office (15 mins), check email/vm (15 mins). Enjoy fruit snack. (Drink water)	
4:45p – 5:15p	30-minute floater.	
5:15p – 5:45p	15-min stand-up staff meeting. Finalize tomorrow's schedule/print.	
5:45p – 7:15p	Drive to the courts, have a great tennis practice!	
7:15p –	Head for home – fun dinner and movie night!	

The Habitually Great "Power Scheduling Habit" is a deliberate Action structure that leads to inspiration. Yet each day and every life are different. Schedule the level of detail that is right for you and fulfills on what you want to accomplish. Ease up on saboteurs like distress or perfection Habits that engage your thoughts with confusion or aggravation about how to do this right. And keep an eye out for any other Limiting Habits that may arise when you start to schedule this way, because as you step into this structure of Right Action and move steadily toward realizing your dreams, old self-sabotaging Habits about worthiness and success may get triggered. Brush them away, shrug them off, or beat them down! In the words of William Shakespeare, "Action is eloquence."

EXERCISE

Do you currently keep a schedule? _____

Where do you keep your schedule? And what do you use (a planner, PDA, wall calendar, legal or note pad, computer software, Internet-based system, your head, etc.)? _____
_____

Have you been scheduling solely work-related items and appointments, or do you also schedule the other areas and roles of your life, too? _____

What scheduling enhancements and Shifts do you want to put into practice? _____
_____
_____

Now identify several key Actions you can take to implement those enhancements and Shifts. List them below and then place them in your schedule for completion, being specific and measurable about what the Actions are, when exactly you will do them, and how much time you will allocate for them. Filter out hiccups, glitches, and any would-be saboteurs like the "Procrastination Habit" that threaten to get in your way. The right time is right now!

Action #1:_____
    I have scheduled to take this Action on/by:_____
    I have allocated (duration): _____
    I fulfilled on this Action on: _____

Action #2:_____
    I have scheduled to take this Action on/by:_____
    I have allocated (duration): _____
    I fulfilled on this Action on: _____

Action #3:_____
    I have scheduled to take this Action on/by:_____
    I have allocated (duration): _____
    I fulfilled on this Action on: _____

And while you're at it, spread the love. Embed discreet reminders in your schedule to practice your "Acknowledgment Habit." Simple touch points—spoken words, written notes, gifts, and such, eliminate feelings of neglect, build trust, and warm the hearts of those around you, yours included.

CHAPTER 8

EMPLOY THE SIMPLEST AND MOST EFFECTIVE DAILY TO-DO SYSTEM

"The materials of action are variable, but the use we make of them should be constant."
—Epictetus

No more sticky notes framed in a random circling pattern on your computer screen or littering your desk, no more legal pads with lists of to-do's—scattered about, or scribbles on paper napkins and business cards. From this point forward, discipline yourself to use just one location for all of your to-do's, one place to keep all of your daily notes and jottings. In that single location, notate the things that come up during the day that you want to, have to, or must do. Choose a to-do receptacle that is convenient to carry and can always be on your person throughout the day, such as a small notepad,

Your printout of today's schedule, or a task list in your mobile device. (I prefer a small spiral pad that fits easily in a jacket, back pack, or pocket.) The caveat is this: from that single source, initiate a regular end-of-day review to move all undone items from your to-do list directly into your schedule, giving each task a scheduled, specific, measurable date and time for completion. No more mile-long lists! After all, anything parked on a list is something that is not being done and has no structure for getting done.)

This may seem a bit radical to you if you think a to-do list is always to be kept separately from your schedule. That productivity structure leads to missed deadlines and forgotten commitments. In a Habitually Great Power Schedule, all tasks are placed into your schedule with specific, measurable dates and timelines for fulfillment. By doing this, you Shift individual tasks into scheduled Actions and completions. (Yes, even for calls, bills, meetings, appointments, research—everything!) This will help you complete important, large, complex, and required tasks as well as quick, easy, discretionary ones.

In addition to this simple, five-minute daily practice, on a weekly basis (pick a regular time for this, such as first thing Monday morning, Friday before leaving work, or Sunday night), perform a look-back, reviewing your daily schedules for the past week. Examine them to ensure all scheduled to-do's from the week were completed, eliminated, or rescheduled. This Right Action step will combat any "Procrastination" or "Sabotage" Habit that may be lurking in the wings.

Melding your to-do list within your schedule creates a synergy that is a Right Action tool for success. If you can't pick a time, you are not going to do it. "Never Doings" will easily identify themselves by their repeated *need* for re-scheduling. On the third reschedule of anything, check in with your "Ground Truth Reality Habit," have a breakthrough,

EMPLOY THE SIMPLEST AND MOST EFFECTIVE DAILY TO-DO SYSTEM

and toss the item out. Monitor your "Can't Say No Habit," interrupt your "Overwhelm Habit," and enjoy the satisfaction of your "Completion Habit." If you have an assistant, you can enhance this structure with a weekly 15-minute meeting together to input all of your tasks (don't leave any unsaid or floating in the back of your mind—download them all), and fine-tune your schedule accordingly.

Are you worried about getting all of this perfectly right? Is that going to stop you from playing with this or picking a small step to implement? If so, that would be a quick and dirty sabotage undermining you. Let's clear perfection off the table.

LIMITING HABIT SPOTLIGHT: THE "PERFECTIONIST HABIT"

If you have one or both sides of the "Perfectionist Habit," you spend a lot of time analyzing and organizing and procrastinating until you are certain that everything is aligned for your success. Perfectionists fall into two categories. One type will start many things yet finish very few. This is because once started, they will only finish something if they can do it exactly right. So this type also has the "Incomplete Habit." A flip side of the "Perfectionist Habit" is the version where they won't even start on a project, goal, or anything if they think they can't do it right. Often this might appear to be the "Procrastination Habit;" look a little closer and see that perfection is at the root.

In Peak Life Habits and Habitually Great programs, we've seen this Habit cause many challenges, including:
1) Inability to settle on a mate, regardless of intention/goal.
2) Consistent dissatisfaction with career, co-workers and others.
3) Either obsessive with fitness/diet or unable to find the right health regimen.

Either side of this Habit can be paralyzing. The "Perfectionist Habit" relies on the "Logic & Justify Habit" for rationalization of why something cannot be done. Yes, a bit of perfectionism in life is a good thing. In this case most Perfectionists will tell you that the Habit runs them and leads to being in a perpetual state of dissatisfaction, both with their lives and with others.

PATTERN INTERRUPT PEAK LIFE HABITS:

Courage Habit, Detachment Habit, I Can Do It Habit, The Right Time Is Right Now Habit, Pattern Interrupt Habit

EMPLOY THE SIMPLEST AND MOST EFFECTIVE DAILY TO-DO SYSTEM

Exercise

Do you keep a to-do list (singular) or to-do lists (plural)? ___

_____

What is the method or are the methods you use for keeping your to-do list(s)? (e.g. paper-based planner, wall calendar, legal or note pad, mobile device, computer-based, Internet/Cloud-based, scrap paper, napkins, sticky notes, your head, etc.): _____

_____

Why have you chosen this system? _____

Where do you keep your to-do list(s)? (e.g. in your briefcase/purse/office computer, on your desk/refrigerator, etc.):

Have you been listing to-dos solely for work or personal-related items, or do you list them for every area of your life? _____

How well is your current to-do system working for you? ___

What, if anything, would you like to change and enhance about current system to help you be more productive, effective, and successful? _____

_____

_____

HABITUALLY GREAT PRODUCTIVITY & TIME MANAGEMENT

Reflect on your answers above and then determine which system you feel will work best for you in the future—one that you will commit to using consistently. Record it here:

_____

_____

Now, how about creating Actions to implement your new system? Identify your first few steps here, schedule them, being specific and measurable, and then complete them!

Action #1: _____
    I have scheduled to take this Action on/by:_____
    I have allocated (duration): _____
    I fulfilled on this Action on: _____

Action #2: _____
    I have scheduled to take this Action on/by:_____
    I have allocated (duration): _____
    I fulfilled on this Action on: _____

Action #3: _____
    I have scheduled to take this Action on/by:_____
    I have allocated (duration): _____
    I fulfilled on this Action on: _____

CHAPTER 9

PREPARE FOR INTERRUPTIONS AND BANISH DISTRACTIONS

"By prevailing over all obstacles and distractions, one may unfailingly arrive at his chosen goal or destination."
—Christopher Columbus

As we are humming through life and work, it is inevitable that we are pulled aside on occasion by interruptions from texts, email, the phone, family, friends, colleagues, customers, vendors, kids, babysitters, others' schedules, and life's unforeseeable events. Despite our best intentions, sometimes it seems that these always prevent us from getting ahead. It's the chaotic Monday morning that greets us after the inspiring weekend workshop or self-help book. The difference is that by the end of this chapter, with your new understanding of what gets in the way, how, and why, you can Shift your perspective and approach during even those disheartening moments.

Accountability, Right Action, and discipline are the powerful tools in your Habitually Great toolbox ready to create results—right now. You and I both know that interruptions and distractions are facts of life, and they happen daily. They may even occupy more of your time than you've been acknowledging. What are your typical interruptions during the course of a day, week, or month? Pull out a pad and pen, and let's make a quick list. Be as honest and specific as possible. Ask yourself questions about your typical day, such as: How much time do I spend on email and the Internet? How much time do I allocate to breaks and meals? How much time do I spend on work and personal phone calls? How much time do I spend daydreaming? How often do I get interrupted or distracted, and for how long?

Tally up those hours and minutes, and let the number sink in. Consider it in comparison to the high quality hours you devote to cultivating your relationships, forwarding your most important projects, and catapulting toward your goals and dreams. Then delve a little deeper to consider which of your Limiting Habits tend to step into the dance during those moments of procrastination, escape, sabotage, avoidance, distraction, interruption, and interference. These are the real culprits! And they offer an excellent opportunity to practice your "Pattern Interrupt Habit."

The first step to engaging the "Pattern Interrupt Habit" is to detach for a moment from the situation. Right Action isn't about being right; it's about being wise and taking Action appropriate to the Outcome you truly want. Note that a Limiting Habit has taken control of the wheel, then select a Peak Life Habit you want to Shift to instead to ensure you get back on track and into Action toward your most desired Outcome.

PREPARE FOR INTERRUPTIONS AND BANISH DISTRACTIONS

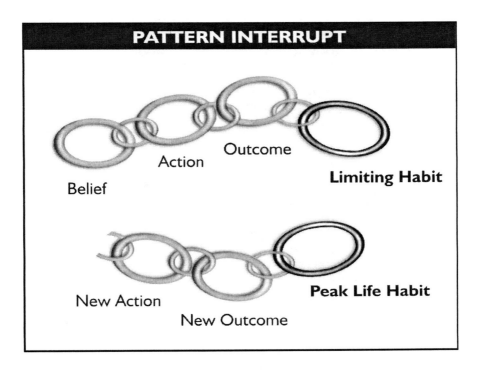

Even the greatest CEOs and Olympians among us are challenged in those moments where they have prepared to take Action, scheduled the Actions, and are in Action. Often, that's when distractions, interruptions, and excuses make an appearance. These will be both aggravating and tempting. Your "Excuses Habit" may pop up along with your "Procrastination," "Distraction/Interruption" and "Struggle" Habits. Then your "Perfectionist Habit" could circulate back again and say, "Wait a minute, is this the right way to do it? I'd better stop." Then your "Logic & Justify Habit" reasons with you, talking you out of Action for a myriad of reasons. Whew! Welcome to the conundrum of Limiting Habits. This is what you are up against every day, and from now on you must overcome those deadbeats and win.

Unfortunately, getting into Action doesn't necessarily circumvent all of them. On most days there may be twenty other things that you could be doing besides what you have planned. You know the feeling: sometimes it is simply an "Overwhelm Habit" triggering you into a circuit overload shutdown as your brain keeps telling you that you have more to do than you can possibly get done. The key to great success is discipline, actually doing what you committed to do while refusing to indulge those old distractions and interruptions. For the most part they aren't forwarding your life or your true happiness. Real contentment is much more satisfying than an in-the-moment distraction.

Here's a classic twist to the distraction scenario to be on the lookout for. Certain Limiting Habits such as the "Fear of Success" and the "I'm Not Great" Habits may take the wheel during those periods of time when things are going well and you're on the verge of achieving a goal you have set. Old ingrained Beliefs in the background may intrude on your path to greatness: "I'm not worthy of this success," "This success can't be real," "I can't keep this up," "This isn't who I really am," etc.

Sunil is a CEO who was overwhelmed running a $250 million dollar company when he sought my help. Like many, Sunil was both successful and unhappy. He had been waiting to be inspired to make changes.. Instead, frustration had clouded his sunny skies. As we discerned together, he did not like being accountable to a schedule; he was used to winging it, a Habit from his early entrepreneurial days. Now he had a list of tasks that was a mile long. There were many things that he had said he would do that he hadn't done. His hours and days were becoming more and more stressful because of this.

Sunil also had a strong "Distraction/Interruption Habit," and it was common for him to drop whatever he was doing whenever someone requested his time. A good example

PREPARE FOR INTERRUPTIONS AND BANISH DISTRACTIONS

was a morning when he was picking up his dry cleaning on the way to work and coincidentally ran into a client. His client expressed an interest in a business chat. Even though Sunil had a fully scheduled day and was already running late, he accommodated his client and agreed to have coffee with him right then at a nearby restaurant. That simple accommodation threw his entire schedule off and exacerbated the stress he was feeling.

A much better alternative would have been to say to his client, "I'd love to talk with you, and my schedule is full for today. I'll have my assistant call you tomorrow to schedule a time for us to get together later in the week. I'm looking forward to it." Why was he so easily derailed?

The first step was to identify and address the Limiting Habits that were getting in his way. It turns out our CEO had a serious confrontation with accountability ("Avoid Accountability Habit" and "Avoid Authority Habit"). He resisted his schedule. He was also controlled by his "Good Person Habit" and his "Can't Say No Habit."

Leaders impact many people. As the leader of his company he saw that his employees often modeled his Habits. His behavior was emulated by the employees throughout his firm. The more organized he could become, the more organized the people around him would become. The better he could become at keeping his word, the better the people around him would become at keeping their word.

A proactive approach to handling distractions and interruptions is applying the Bucket of Time exercise to identify exactly how much time in a day you want to *allocate* for interruptions. Most of us are not budgeting enough time for these, and so we tap daily into our "Frustration Habit" instead of our "Power Scheduling Habit." Scheduling well requires applying the principles of your "Ground Truth Reality Habit," authentically seeing and dealing with the reality of your life. If you are interrupted on average two hours per day, schedule for those interruptions and stop complaining about them! Interrupt your "Victim Habit" about interruptions and start looking at how to change their pattern so that you control how and when they occur.

Peter owned a landscape contracting business that was very successful. He prided himself on his great installers and his one-on-one interaction with his customers. Here's the paradox: Peter used to react angrily every time his phone rang, occasionally even throwing the phone and cursing at it. He was frustrated with the interruptions of that phone during his workday. However, the callers were his customers. The irony is if his phone didn't ring randomly and sporadically, he wouldn't be able to pay for his house, cars, food, clothes, healthcare, fishing trips, or children's education. Those were paying customers old and new calling.

We reworked his perspective, changed his voicemail message so that he communicated clearly about when he would return those calls and redirected many of them to his assistant. Here's the most interesting part: we clarified that the calls weren't interruptions at all. Rather, they were part of his job description. Even though he had told clients to call the office, he'd also given them his cell phone number. He hadn't looked at it that way because his "Victim Habit" had insisted on being front and center with his internal and external voices saying that the calls were frustrating intrusions. That Limiting Habit had been stamped into his subconscious a long, long time ago.

Applying the Buckets of Time exercise to your distractions and interruptions allows you to *recognize* and *manage* them. Being aware of the interruptions and distractions that are an inevitable part of everyone's daily life will help to alleviate

PREPARE FOR INTERRUPTIONS AND BANISH DISTRACTIONS

feelings of resentment, overwhelm, and even depression. This will go a long way toward creating a schedule that accommodates them and Shifts those moments so that you manage them, instead of letting them manage you.

If you want to make speedy progress toward Shifting your perspective on and approach to interruptions and distractions, consider implementing some or all of the following tips:

1. *Do Not Disturb:* Change your "Open Door Habit" at work (and at home, too) by interrupting your "Distraction/Interruption Habit" and perhaps your "Need To Be Needed Habit." Create or order a sign to hang on your door that reads "Please Knock First Before Entering" or "Working—Do Not Disturb."

2. *Solitary Work Blocks:* Create scheduled solitary work blocks to catch up, focus, and catapult. This means having a breakthrough in your "Saying No Authentically Habit," closing the door, turning off the phone, shutting down the email, and digging into your top priorities. A time span of between two-to-four hours often works best, and 30 minutes is a great start too!

3. *Answering The Phone:* At work or at home, when you answer your phone, give a warm greeting, and then follow it by stating an immediate time-boundary expectation: "I'm glad you called! Unfortunately, I can only spare about five minutes now; will that be enough time, or do we want to schedule for a longer call?" or "I know this is an important topic to cover, let's schedule a good time when we can discuss it at leisure."

HABITUALLY GREAT PRODUCTIVITY & TIME MANAGEMENT

4. *Authentic & Compassionate:* Express your feelings with compassion if you feel that you are not being recognized or heard: "Listen, I'm here for you, and I understand the importance of this to you. It's just that right now I've got to stay on task. Let's find the perfect time to discuss this together; how does later today or tomorrow look for your schedule?" Be firm and powerful in your words (surprise yourself) by using your "Authentic" with "Compassion" Habits.

5. *Keep Your Word:* Be accountable to the time commitments you make so that others develop trust and respect for what you say. Use your "Keeping My Word Habit" while establishing parameters that work. People will learn from you and model the "Integrity Habit" you are demonstrating!

6. *Say "No":* Substitute your "Good Person" and "Can't Say No," Habits with your "Accountability," "Discipline" and "Saying No Authentically" Habits. Actually, when you apply Tips 2 and 3, others will find your heartfelt "Compassion Habit" more open and generous, because your "Resentment" and "Victim" Habits have been pre-empted by your "Authentic Habit." You will feel happier and that will rub off on those around you.

7. *Transform Big Tasks to Bite Sized:* When a big task or a multitude of to-do's triggers your "Overwhelm Habit" and you launch into a pattern of distraction/interruption, simplify immediately. Take a big task and make it into something small and manageable. Keep shrinking it until there's something you can do within a reasonable time frame. Transcend and narrow large tasks by cutting them

PREPARE FOR INTERRUPTIONS AND BANISH DISTRACTIONS

into small pieces first and then just focusing on completing one small, doable piece at a time.

8. *Checking Email:* Start your day without looking at email first. Instead look at your schedule and dig in. Spend at least 30–60 minutes each day getting organized and launching into the important Actions scheduled for the day. Then schedule an email check. Additionally, effective immediately, turn your email alarms off and immediately stop randomly checking email. Schedule 15-minute blocks of time for checking and responding to email, based on a ground truth analysis of what is most effective and efficient for executing your priorities while being appropriately responsive. Also, set clear guidelines for people so they know they can count on you to respond to email at regular intervals—for instance, every three hours or by day's end.

9. *Text Messaging, Social Media, Mobile Apps:* Repeat Tip 8 for text messaging, social media, and mobile apps. If you have created the expectation that you are available and can respond throughout the day, change that now. This is another insidious form of distraction. Set clear guidelines and boundaries for people who are in your communication networks. Solitary work blocks (Tip 2) are best done without interruptions of any kind!

EXERCISE

What types of interruptions tend to interfere with your schedule on a typical day?

- _____
- _____
- _____
- _____
- _____

Sometimes we distract ourselves, especially when we have too much to do and feel overwhelmed, when things are going well, and even when we are very close to achieving the goals we have set. What has been the typical manifestation of your "Distraction," "Procrastination," "Escape," "Self-Sabotage" and/or "Avoidance" Habits?

- _____
- _____
- _____
- _____
- _____

Which of your Limiting Habits participates in moments of interruption and distraction?

- _____
- _____
- _____

PREPARE FOR INTERRUPTIONS AND BANISH DISTRACTIONS

And, most importantly, which Peak Life Habits will you commit to substituting so in the future you can preempt your interruptions and distractions?

- _____
- _____
- _____

CHAPTER 10

CARVE OUT SOLITARY WORK BLOCKS WITH NO INTERRUPTIONS

"Concentrate all your thoughts on the task at hand. The sun's rays do not burn until brought to a focus."
—Alexander Graham Bell

How often do you feel overwhelmed by distractions and interruptions? This next exercise challenges you to carve out blocks of solitary work time on a regular basis where you will allow no interruptions or distractions to get in the way of making major strides in your productivity.

An uninterrupted time span of from two to four hours often works best. We want to create these work blocks so we can focus, catch up, and hasten the completion of our most important projects and goals. This means achieving a breakthrough on closing the door, turning off the phone, shutting down e-mail, and digging into the work at hand. This also means building the appropriate leadership muscle of saying "No" for short periods of time.

Recognize that during these blocks, Limiting Habits could make completing your task a challenge. The "Need To Be Needed" and "Good Person" Habits are typical saboteurs. Consider this is a great opportunity, then, not only to get work done but to further practice your "Pattern Interrupt Habit" whenever the need arises, so you can get into—and stay in—your peak performance zone.

We all want to become better disciplined at carving out blocks of solitary time for ourselves so we can push key initiatives forward. An additional benefit you will likely discover is that when you start consistently creating solitary work blocks with no interruptions, you will find yourself gaining more respect from others. Even when you don't answer a phone call or an e-mail immediately, everything will work out well.

CARVE OUT SOLITARY WORK BLOCKS WITH NO INTERRUPTIONS

EXERCISE

In the coming week, carve out at least two blocks of solitary work time. Ideally, schedule these blocks to extend from two to four hours. Or, if this seems too challenging, begin with a 60 or 90 minute work block. During these periods, close your door, switch your phone over to voicemail, and place an automatic reply on your e-mail that states, "I'm on a work block right now; I'll get back to you _____ (this afternoon, etc.)." If need be, flex your "Saying No Authentically Habit," and consider hanging a "Do Not Disturb!" sign on the doorknob. Then dive straight work at hand.

Solitary Work Block #1
Date:_____ Time:_____ Duration:_____

Solitary Work Block #2
Date:_____ Time:_____ Duration:_____

While working, make sure to preempt or Shift any Limiting Habits that pop up, threatening to derail progress. And take note of these would-be saboteurs for future reference. Also note the Peak Life Habits to which you Shift that help you to better protect your solitary work block.

HABITUALLY GREAT PRODUCTIVITY & TIME MANAGEMENT

What Limiting Habits during this time did you find yourself Shifting or circumventing?

- _____
- _____
- _____

What Peak Life Habits did you Shift to?

- _____
- _____
- _____

What else did you do to protect this time? And did you feel less overwhelmed? Did the world manage to survive without you for those hours? Describe what happened and how you felt. _____
_____
_____
_____
_____

What were you able to accomplish? _____
_____
_____

CARVE OUT SOLITARY WORK BLOCKS WITH NO INTERRUPTIONS

In the future, what improvements can you make to this exercise so that great and uninterrupted Solitary Work Blocks become a productive new Peak Life Habit for you? _____

_____
_____
_____
_____

Always strive to manage time in alignment with your true priorities. Remember, it's up to you to allocate the 24 hours in a day. There will never be less or more, so design your schedule to complete your projects, achieve your goals, and realize your dreams!

CHAPTER 11

NAIL DOWN YOUR STOP DOING LIST

"We always have time enough, if we will but use it aright."
—Johann Wolfgang Von Goethe

One of the keys to creating a realistic schedule is to generate a Stop Doing list. In many respects technology has increased the pace of our lives—not our happiness. With the ramp-up of high-speed communication, there are very few moments we have to ourselves. Even children today are bombarded with the demands of a world that is always busy with communication; kids can't take their bikes out for a spin without a helmet *and* a cell phone. With this communication invasion has come a rapid expansion of to-do's. The requests on our time are endless. To master Right Action you must take that deep breath and start saying "No." Your health, happiness, and success are at stake. You know those roles, projects, and tasks that no longer fit with your plan for greatness. To cross the chasm of the Habit-Gap, you must take the Right Action and stop doing them!

Here is the key question: once you know the Right Action, do you have the discipline to take it? Defeat all the old Limiting Habits that have been stopping you from stopping! Are you ready to stop doing at least a few of those things that give you little joy, really aren't that important, can be done by someone else, or are being done simply because of Limiting Habits like the "Good Person," "Drama," "Domination & Control," "Do It Myself," "Looking Good," or "Obsess" Habits?

It is time to create a Stop Doing List using your "Ground Truth Reality Habit," and then follow through with putting an end to everything on that list. Which distractions and interruptions will you refuse to allow? What activities and Actions will you courageously quit? Clear the highway to *Positively Inspiring Success* by taking Right Action, and cease and desist from everything that has been holding you back from reaching your goals and fulfilling your most important commitments, and anything that has been leaving you feeling resentful or exhausted.

Following through on this next exercise is going to be fun, because it will leave you feeling refreshed and vibrant. In fact, you may find yourself feeling so terrific you opt to maintain a Stop Doing List on a consistent basis and keep adding outdated Actions and obligations that no longer align with your Habitually Great life, carting all those items off to the junkyard. If the "Can't Say No Habit" has been a problem for you in the past, creating and maintaining a Stop Doing List will help you circumvent it and give you excellent practice in building a strong, healthy "Saying No Authentically Habit."

LIMITING HABIT SPOTLIGHT: THE "CAN'T SAY NO HABIT"

We field requests all day and every day from a multitude of sources. In the midst of those we find ourselves saying "Yes" to so many things that there isn't a prayer that we will achieve and accomplish what we've said "Yes" to. And once the overwhelm sets in, we are stuck feeling like the hamster on the wheel, round and round and round we go with no way off.

The "Can't Say No Habit" often goes hand-in-hand with a life and a schedule that is too busy, overwhelming, exhausting, etc. Most of us have a slice of this Limiting Habit, and it has a remarkable impact in disrupting our plans to accomplish what we say we want.

Become an expert at saying "No" so that you can say "Yes" powerfully. With the proper language skills, we can become experts at saying "No" while still leaving everybody happy, including ourselves. A simple practice to start now is to say "No" to spontaneous requests for your time and compassionately schedule an appropriate meeting time instead.

Being powerful in saying "No" is as important as being powerful in saying "Yes." Saying "No" authentically is a positive committed expression spoken with clarity and truth, for example: "I'd like to help, and No, I'm sorry, I won't be able to do that." Everyone is better off when they communicate "No" with kind, straightforward honesty. After all, how many times has your Pleaser Habit had you say "Yes" to things you either did not want to do or did not follow through with?

Is your "Can't Say No Habit" burning fires in your schedule? Are you sidetracked by all kinds of interruptions? Take a deep breath and say these words: "I am really buried right now, let's schedule a good time to meet." (That is a kind way of saying "Not right now.")

We respect people who say no. Their integrity draws a clear line, and we trust their "No" and their "Yes." This makes it very easy to communicate and work together. Adapt that style for yourself too, and you will earn greater appreciation and respect from everyone in your life. Oh, and you will be much happier.

PATTERN INTERRUPT PEAK LIFE HABITS:

Saying No Authentically Habit, Putting Myself First Habit, Ground Truth Habit, Power Scheduling Habit, Stop Doing Habit

Another bonus from creating your list and following through by practicing your "Saying No Authentically Habit," is that you'll soon find yourself in the position of being able to say yes even more powerfully. For the moment, though, let's zero in on what you're going to put an end to. And while you work through this exercise, consider this tip: for those items involving others, remember that you will want to contact whoever will be impacted by your decisions. Schedule those communications, and as you do, make sure to include your intended Outcomes, too. You will enjoy seeing what happens during the actual moments. Above all, though, follow through, and hold yourself accountable for creating some great breathing space in your life and schedule.

NAIL DOWN YOUR STOP DOING LIST

EXERCISE

1. I am going to Stop Doing:_____

The Action I've added to my schedule to make sure I follow through is: _____

_____

I will Stop Doing this: A. Immediately_____

or B: As of this date:_____

I will contact the following person(s) to inform them of this:

_____

2. I am going to Stop Doing: _____

The Action I've added to my schedule to make sure I follow through is: _____

_____

I will Stop Doing this: A. Immediately_____

or B: As of this date:_____

I will contact the following person(s) to inform them of this:

_____

3. I am going to Stop Doing: _____

The Action I've added to my schedule to make sure I follow through is: _____

_____

I will Stop Doing this: A. Immediately_____

or B: As of this date:_____

I will contact the following person(s) to inform them of this:
_____

4. I am going to Stop Doing: _____

The Action I've added to my schedule to make sure I follow through is: _____

_____

I will Stop Doing this: A. Immediately_____
or B: As of this date:_____
I will contact the following person(s) to inform them of this:
_____

CHAPTER 12

DREAM UP YOUR START DOING LIST

"Do not wait; the time will never be "just right." Start where you stand, and work with whatever tools you may have at your command, and better tools will be found as you go along."
—Napoleon Hill

You have the journey for the next leg of your trip sketched out and your navigation system is programmed. The superhighway of Right Action has now been illuminated, and you may already love being on it. In other words, you may have already set your enhanced or new intentions in motion, created or adopted some practices of Habitually Great Power Scheduling, crafted or implemented your Stop Doing List, and you're eager for more. It's time, then, for the "Saying Yes Powerfully Habit." This Habit will help you to leverage your expanded productivity and Right Action Habits by applying them to even more of your desires.

You may also want to leverage your new productivity and Right Action Habits by resolving old commitments and some of your incomplete To-Do's. Areas that are incomplete in our lives take up important bandwidth in our heads, too. A simple practice is to list up to 10 areas of your life where you have made lingering and unresolved commitments—unfinished business, so to speak. Pick the easiest five and schedule the Actions that will tie up the loose ends and complete them. A few authentic "No's" can go a long way toward clearing out the congestion. You will feel clearer, stronger and more focused on your future once you resolve the issues and incomplete commitments that have been weighing on your mind today. What Limiting Habits have kept those in circulation? It is your accountability to preempt those and clear the space for your ultimate life!

The greatness of your life happens with luck, with love, with intentional discipline and perseverance, nose to the grindstone, patiently smiling, knowing that your inspiration will arrive and desired outcomes will spring to life. With the following exercise, we'll focus on exciting new initiatives that align with your evolved vision of your life.

Now is the right time to throw your hat in the ring and get started. What are you going to Start Doing? (Remember, the Right Time is Right Now!)

DREAM UP YOUR START DOING LIST

EXERCISE

1. I am going to Start: _____

_____

The Action I've added to my schedule to make sure I follow through is: _____

_____

I will Start this: A. Immediately _____
or B: As of this date: _____
I will contact the following person(s) to inform them of this:

_____

2. I am going to Start: _____

_____

The Action I've added to my schedule to make sure I follow through is: _____

_____

I will Start this: A. Immediately _____
or B: As of this date: _____
I will contact the following person(s) to inform them of this:

_____

3. I am going to Start: _____

_____

The Action I've added to my schedule to make sure I follow through is: _____

I will Start this: A. Immediately _____

or B: As of this date: _____

I will contact the following person(s) to inform them of this:

_____

4. I am going to Start: _____

The Action I've added to my schedule to make sure I follow through is: _____

I will Start this: A. Immediately _____

or B: As of this date: _____

I will contact the following person(s) to inform them of this:

_____

CHAPTER 13

TAKE ON THE "CONFRONTATION WITH BEING COMPLETE HABIT"

> *"Overcome your inertia. Since to be inert is to be without action, agree to become a being of movement: Plan to exercise, make that call you've been avoiding, or write that letter . . . . Experience the apprehension and do it anyway! It's the doing that brings you to a new level of inspiration."*
> —Dr. Wayne W. Dyer

If you have a strong drive toward maintaining a sense of independence and spontaneity, make sure that these desires don't bar the way to resolving outstanding issues. These inclinations could be masking deeper fears—of completion and ultimately, even, success. For when we refuse to allow ourselves to experience the feeling of completion, we also refuse ourselves the joy of achievement. This in turn prevents us from becoming more productive, skyrocketing forward, and accomplishing either simple or far-reaching objectives. Yet we sometimes unconsciously adopt this Limiting Habit because then we don't have to deal with consistently managing the results of our achievements and the expectations we believe our successes would create.

If you suspect this may be an occasional or perpetual issue for you, then take it on here and now. Dispatch with your "Confrontation With Being Complete Habit" in this next exercise. Rise out of the quicksand and make powerful headway!

TAKE ON THE "CONFRONTATION WITH BEING COMPLETE HABIT"

EXERCISE

My definition of completion is: _____
_____

My definition of success is: _____
_____

I am uncomfortable with or intimidated by completion, because: _____
_____

I am comfortable leaving loose ends, because: _____
_____

If completing an objective leads to success, I may perceive a discomfort about maintaining that success in the future. It makes me fearful, because: _____
_____

When I am confronted with completion, organizing myself in order to complete something, or scheduling to complete or fulfill on something, I feel: _____
_____

A loose end/issue/goal I want to complete is: _____
_____

HABITUALLY GREAT PRODUCTIVITY & TIME MANAGEMENT

This week, come to completion with this issue. Determine what Actions will be necessary, then list and schedule them. Complete them one by one and note here when you finish each. Also remember to monitor your Limiting Habits and adopt any Peak Life Habits that will help you complete each Action step.

Action #1:_____
    I have scheduled to take this Action on/by:_____
    I have allocated (duration): _____
    I fulfilled on this Action on: _____

Action #2:_____
    I have scheduled to take this Action on/by:_____
    I have allocated (duration): _____
    I fulfilled on this Action on: _____

Action #3:_____
    I have scheduled to take this Action on/by:_____
    I have allocated (duration): _____
    I fulfilled on this Action on: _____

TAKE ON THE "CONFRONTATION WITH BEING COMPLETE HABIT"

END-OF-THE-WEEK REVIEW

If you succeeded at facing your "Confrontation With Being Complete Habit" during the week and achieved your goal, describe how that made you feel.

When I actually completed on this issue, I felt: _____

I believe this key Peak Life Habit helped me to succeed: _

If you weren't able to complete on this issue, explain why you think this was the case, and describe how this made you feel.

I didn't complete and fulfill on this issue, because: _____

I believe this key Limiting Habit held me back:_____

Having failed to complete on this issue, I feel: _____

What am I going to do about it?_____

CHAPTER 14

PRACTICE REVERSE TIMELINE SCHEDULING

"Planning is bringing the future into the present so that you can do something about it now."
—Alan Lakein

Reverse Timeline Scheduling offers the opportunity to articulate all the steps or milestones you want to achieve along the way to an Outcome you are passionate about. It is the rapid transit system of fulfilled Outcomes by deconstructing your schedule from the end to the beginning. Each step is clarified, invoked, and scheduled for Action. The magic is in working backwards—from your last Action step marking completion of your objective to the first step along the path. The path revealed will lay out the Actions that lead straight to success. This approach to your life truly fulfills on beginning with the end in mind.

HABITUALLY GREAT PRODUCTIVITY & TIME MANAGEMENT

Reverse Timeline Scheduling is a nifty and straightforward mechanism that also aligns perfectly with accountability, specificity, and measurability. This is how you take your life's successes from random to deliberate. Complex long-term and straightforward short-term objectives are sliced and diced into easy bite-sized pieces, then scheduled and fulfilled. *Voila*, you will arrive at the intersection where your destiny meets Right Action.

The exercise ahead, is your invitation—and opportunity!—to get started building this new Peak Life Habit. First, you will choose an objective, take a few minutes to do some Imagineering, and then map out your path of Right Action on the Reverse Timeline template provided. Next, you will chart your path's coordinates in your schedule. And finally, you will want to fill up your tank with motivational fuel, hit the gas pedal, and take off toward your first Milestone marker!

Before you begin, though, a few tips will help you get the most out of this success structure. If there are any Actions you find yourself unsure of, make sure to schedule for research time, as well as preparation and follow through. Also, once you have begun to put your plan into play, if you spot a "Perfectionist Habit" jumping into the fray, give it a hall pass. Be bold; refuse to allow old Limiting Habits to stop you from taking persistent daily Action, pushing the ball forward with vim and vigor, and making touchdown after touchdown. Also, if at any point you feel uncertain, trust that all the Right Actions necessary to secure your Outcome will reveal themselves—as long as you keep moving ahead. As you follow your plan, remember to remain flexible as well. Always be willing to revise your program as new information, obstacles, or unforeseen opportunities arise. When they do (and if your goal has any level of complexity, you can pretty much count on it!), simply reschedule any missed Action steps or revise the plan to accommodate the new opportunities,

PRACTICE REVERSE TIMELINE SCHEDULING

accordingly—with intentional timelines. Then dive back into Action to fulfill them, and be sure to enjoy the exhilaration of building momentum with every step taken along the road to success!

EXERCISE

My Intention or Outcome/ is: _____

_____

The exact date by which I will accomplish it is: _____

_____

On a separate pad or worksheet, in bullet form, do some Imagineering and articulate randomly, as they come to mind, different Action steps you may want to take and milestones you may want to reach en route in to your desired destination. Be specific, though: include any phone calls, conversations, research, applications, classes, training sessions, tournaments, you name it, whatever it will take to produce the desired Outcome. When you feel confident that you have exhausted your imagination on this score—are sure you have captured all the Actions and milestones you believe necessary to achieving your goal—take a few deep breaths and relax for a moment.

Now, it's time to put your "Focus & Clarity" and "Specific & Measurable" Habits into play! Working backwards from your desired date of fulfillment, organize your list of objectives by determining and committing to realistic due dates for each Action and milestone. Remember, the key to creating your Reverse Timeline is to schedule each step in reverse order, working back step by step from your completion date and last milestone or Action to the first. A tip: placing all these points along your path to success into your schedule would be a great "Today" Action.

PRACTICE REVERSE TIMELINE SCHEDULING

REVERSE TIMELINE SCHEDULE

Outcome Achieved By: _____

Date: _____ Milestone/Action 10: _____
Date: _____ Milestone/Action 9: _____
Date: _____ Milestone/Action 8: _____
Date: _____ Milestone/Action 7: _____
Date: _____ Milestone/Action 6: _____
Date: _____ Milestone/Action 5: _____
Date: _____ Milestone/Action 4: _____
Date: _____ Milestone/Action 3: _____
Date: _____ Milestone/Action 2: _____
Date: _____ Milestone/Action 1: _____

Finally, flex your "The Right Time Is Right Now Habit" muscle by taking my tip: place each Action and milestone in your schedule. Fire up your engine and get rolling toward your goal by taking your first Action step today! Then be sure to keep your engine running by applying your "Discipline" and "Patience" Habits to this RTS success structure, while fulfilling every Action on your list. No matter how low on energy or nervous you many feel, no matter what excuses you may be tempted to make, take the Actions you have committed to at the appointed hours! Also be sure to monitor and cast aside any interruptions, distractions, or other more covert forms of sabotage that threaten to slow your progress or throw you off course. If you blow a deadline, just put your "Living In Reality" and "Lightening Up" Habits into play; reschedule the missed Actions and fulfill them. Step by step, momentum will build and you will achieve your Outcome!

CHAPTER 15

BUILD TEAMWORK BY MASTERING THE ART OF DELEGATION

"If your actions inspire others to dream more, learn more, do more, and become more, you are a leader."
—John Quincy Adams

In most aspects of our lives, we rely on others to help us achieve our goals. One Peak Life Habit that maximizes your performance in many of your roles is The "Teamwork Habit." Every day you start and finish countless "mini-teams" as your life's path intersects with others: in a traffic jam, at the doctor's office, in a meeting or classroom, on a social networking website, even at a restaurant. Being part of those ad hoc teams is just the beginning. You also, of course, are a part of more formal groupings—in your family, friendships, work environment, community, and perhaps even on a sports team. Your happiness and success are inexorably linked to your skills at teamwork. Build trust and vanquish Limiting Habits such as the "Doing it My Way" and "I'm Right" Habits. Teamwork and effective delegation are the gold keys to your larger dreams.

The foundation of the "Teamwork Habit" is trust. Not blind trust, rather the trust of knowing that just about everyone is capable and has good smarts, even as they also possess their unique bundle of Peak Life and Limiting Habits, just like you. Allow yourself some wisdom here; discern what Habits others on your teams have and recognize how those Habits will impact your teamwork. This is your responsibility, and it disengages your "Seeing What's Wrong Habit" so that you deploy that Habit only for data-gathering and other similarly constructive purposes. Is there a team you're on where trust is broken or seriously impeded? If so, and if you want it repaired, you must U-turn your finger. Ask yourself honestly how you participated in creating the breakdown. What could you have done differently that would have led to a more positive result? Here's an interesting nuance: if you don't trust a situation, group, or individual, trust them not to be trustworthy. Because trusting people to be who they are and who they are not gives you a lot of freedom. Then you can stop playing the victim to your repeatedly unfulfilled expectations, and do something a lot more powerful!

Some teams we are on are not by choice, rather by circumstance; for example, those with our parents, siblings, and kids, and even some with our colleagues or classmates. Our accountability with those teams is both to be responsible for our own Habits and to be wise, compassionate, and preemptive about theirs. There are also many teams we purposefully select and build, including our marriages. In all cases, participate on your teams with compassion and wisdom, using the balance of your "Being Appropriate" and "Authentic" Habits. Hold yourself accountable and manage your "Cut & Run Habit" while at the same time improving or changing your teams when there is a mismatch. Summon up your "Ground Truth Reality Habit," then select teammates and create teams well, always taking Right Action with them to fulfill on your goals and happiness!

Let's turn the spotlight now on an important Habit that blends synergistically with the "Teamwork Habit"—the "Effective Delegation Habit," a Peak Life Habit that empowers others to succeed while simultaneously maximizing your teamwork and time management skills.

PEAK LIFE HABIT SPOTLIGHT:
The "Effective Delegation Habit"

An important element of Right Action is to become a great conductor of communication and delegation. Though many of us have a dominant "I'm Alone Habit," we are always interacting with others. As an effective delegator, you can achieve many more of your desires. Empowering others to succeed benefits everyone. Whether you are a team member, an executive, or a parent, mastering the art of delegation can elevate your and others' happiness and success to wonderful new heights.

Effective delegation involves more than just good communication. It requires the Peak Life Habits of *"Setting People Up To Be Successful Habit," "Setting People Up To Be Powerful Habit, "Trusting Others Habit,"* and more.

An important key to great delegation is mastery of the following eight steps, many of which are excerpted from Donna Genett's wise book on the same subject entitled: *If You Want It Done Right, You Don't Have To Do It Yourself*. Apply this practice immediately and enjoy real breakthroughs in teamwork, trust, communication, and happiness. This is a pre-emptive, practical way of communicating that can create exceptional results.

1. Prepare beforehand—know exactly what your task or request is.
2. Together, clearly define the task or request to be completed.
3. Agree to a specific timeframe for the delegated task.
4. Clarify the level of authority you are assigning for this task.
5. Identify checkpoints that are specific, measurable, and clear.
6. Afterwards, debrief together and identify ways to improve the process.
7. U-Turn your finger—make sure you are setting people up to succeed.
8. Enact appropriate consequences when the delegatee misses commitments.

Follow the nuances of this communication model in many areas of your life, with clients, staff, family, etc., and you will notice great outcomes and joy! Monitor yourself for setting people up to fail—keep your "Domination & Control Habit" and other Limiting Habits listed below out of this game.

The "Effective Delegation Habit" Interrupts:

I'm Right Habit, Making People Feel Bad Habit, I Can Do It Better & Faster Habit, I Don't Trust Habit, Seeing What's Wrong Habit.

BUILD TEAMWORK BY MASTERING THE ART OF DELEGATION

Together, the "Teamwork Habit" and the "Effective Delegation Habit" can supercharge your life while building relationships that are founded on the "Being Powerful" and the "Humility" Habits. Recognize the strengths of others as you acknowledge and ask for assistance in areas in which you are uncertain or weak. Build great teams in all areas of life and work, and you will climb the highest peaks, individually and together!

EXERCISE

At which of the eight steps do you already excel in the delegation process? _____
_____

Do you think you perform better as a delegator or a delegatee? Why? _____
_____

Which of your Limiting Habits threaten to get in the way of a smooth delegation process?
- _____
- _____
- _____

Which of these steps can you use to improve the way you delegate and manage projects, tasks, and issues?
_____
_____

If you practice the "Effective Delegation Habit" by following this eight-step process, do you think that the results of projects, tasks, and issues you delegate will improve? Why?
_____
_____

What past delegation experience(s) could have been improved had you used this process?

_____
_____

Which of your currently delegated projects, tasks, and issues could you manage more effectively now that you understand successful delegation and delegation pitfalls?

_____
_____

What are you currently doing yourself that would be better delegated so you can focus on more important areas with your time (at work, at home, etc.)?

_____
_____

Which Peak Life Habits will you now commit to using as your guiding modes for attaining top-notch communication and supporting your "Effective Delegation Habit," as well as being a great participant when you are the delegatee?

- _____
- _____
- _____

CHAPTER 16

BE GREAT AT YOUR JOB!

"Gather in your resources, rally all your faculties, marshal all your energies, focus all your capacities upon mastery of at least one field of endeavor."
—John Haggai

As you increase your mastery of time management, scheduling, and staying in Right Action, once in a while your Limiting Habits are predictably going to step in the roadway. In those moments, smile knowingly, and then get right back to taking the power, staying in Action. Shift to the "Focus & Clarity Habit" and you will be so organized that you will no longer even have to worry about being organized.

Remember, Habitual Greatness is fun! Play with it in every area of your life—not least in your career. Whatever your position—be it a work-at-home mom with one or more children to raise, a mid-level manager, a community activist, an entrepreneur, a research scientist, a student, athlete, artist or musician, a CEO on a variety of boards, you name it—play with being a peak performer, modeling standout behavior, achieving top-notch results, and just enjoying the integrity of doing and being your best every day on the job!

In honor of this, let's do one more exercise together before we part ways. Here our aim will be to support our efforts to reach a new peak in our careers by choosing to memorialize in writing the milestones we're committed to achieving. This is one final success structure to add to the mix. Staying committed to this practice, along with our other Peak Life Habits, will help clear the path forward to ever greater success!

EXERCISE

What's next—the next rung, big step, position, etc., in your career? _____

_____

Determine how you will measure success for that position, and then list these core measurements that will confirm that the success has been reached.

- _____
- _____
- _____

Given the information listed above, focus intently on several of the stepping-stone goals along the path to your career objective above and capture them here. (Remember to apply your "Specific & Measurable Habit"!) Then determine and schedule the Actions you will take to achieve each of these goals and, most importantly, fulfill on them.

Goal #1: _____

Related data points & details:

- _____
- _____
- _____

Action: _____
- I have scheduled to take this Action on/by:_____
- I have allocated (duration): _____
- I fulfilled on this Action on: _____

Action: _____
- I have scheduled to take this Action on/by:_____
- I have allocated (duration): _____
- I fulfilled on this Action on: _____

Action: _____
- I have scheduled to take this Action on/by:_____
- I have allocated (duration): _____
- I fulfilled on this Action on: _____

Goal #2:_____
Related data points & details:
- _____
- _____
- _____

Action: _____
- I have scheduled to take this Action on/by:_____
- I have allocated (duration): _____
- I fulfilled on this Action on: _____

Action: _____
- I have scheduled to take this Action on/by:_____
- I have allocated (duration): _____
- I fulfilled on this Action on: _____

Action: _____
- I have scheduled to take this Action on/by:_____
- I have allocated (duration): _____
- I fulfilled on this Action on: _____

Goal #3:_____
Related data points & details:
- _____
- _____
- _____

Action: _____
- I have scheduled to take this Action on/by:_____
- I have allocated (duration): _____
- I fulfilled on this Action on: _____

Action: _____
- I have scheduled to take this Action on/by:_____
- I have allocated (duration): _____
- I fulfilled on this Action on: _____

Action: _____
- I have scheduled to take this Action on/by: _____
- I have allocated (duration): _____
- I fulfilled on this Action on: _____

Considering the Actions you've scheduled, identify the Limiting Habits most likely to challenge your discipline. And for each little saboteur you identify, choose a Peak Life Habit to which you will commit to Shifting when the Limiting Habit threatens to slow your progress or bump you off the path to your goals.

Limiting Habits you Shift to Peak Life Habits:
Limiting Habit #1: _____
    Shifts to Peak Life Habit: _____
Limiting Habit #2: _____
    Shifts to Peak Life Habit: _____
Limiting Habit #3: _____
    Shifts to Peak Life Habit: _____

Remember, Shifting to your Peak Life Habits will help facilitate and ramp up your "Discipline" and "Self-Accountability" Habits, which in turn will catapult you toward your goals, pre-empt every "Distraction Habit" and "Interruption Habit" that threatens to get in your way, and keep you in powerful Action!

CONCLUSION

PUTTING IT ALL TOGETHER

Here is a summary of the 16 principles of Habitually Great Time Management and Productivity. Review these regularly—perhaps on a weekly basis—until they become thoroughly ingrained in your Beliefs, Actions, and Habits, and your *Positively Inspiring Success* is assured. Remember those big dreams, intentions, changes, and contributions you outlined at the beginning of our work together? Practicing these golden rules on a daily basis will give you license to consider them a done deal!

1. **Infuse Your Life with Right Action:** Be respectful and appreciative of yourself and others. Take positive, disciplined, persistent Action with clarity, focus, specificity, and measurability. This is the most effective antidote to the poison of Limiting Habits. It also reinforces and strengthens your commitment to desired Outcomes.

2. **Draw Your Inspiration from Discipline:** Habitual Greatness is about taking sustained Right Action day in and day out. Set up a schedule to accomplish your objectives and then follow through. Create structures of discipline and accountability for yourself and stick to them with absolute persistence, regardless of how you're feeling. Discipline and persistence will pave your way to amazing breakthroughs and *Positively Inspiring Success*!

3. **Put the "Right Action Momentum Habit" into Play:** Most great achievements begin as mere ideas with little muscle mass to support them. Use the initial push and continuing discipline that come from putting the "Right Action Momentum Habit" into play in your life. Even if old Limiting Habits cause you to stumble off the path on occasion, this Habit will help you recover the ground quickly and power forward. Your intentions will gain mass and momentum, leading you to grow, develop, and ascend.

4. **Get Clear on Your Multiple Roles in Life:** Most of us have at least five or more basic life areas with roles that are best served by scheduling appropriate Actions and time for them. Move further into living Habitual Greatness by identifying your key areas of commitment and responsibility, setting goals for each one of them, and then doing whatever it takes to give them their full due in your schedule and life.

5. **Appreciate that Time Is Just Time:** We all have the same 24 hours in a day 365 days a year. It's only a matter of how much Right Action we take during those hours, days, and years that determines our level of greatness,

PUTTING IT ALL TOGETHER

success, and happiness. Refuse to justify unrealized goals and intentions due to time constraints. Say to yourself daily: "Time is just time!" Then, if necessary, alter your relationship to and prioritize your time in the manner that best supports your relationships, joys, and life's intentions.

6. **Fill Your Buckets of Time with Pure Gold:** Whenever you find yourself feeling frustrated and wondering how time and your goals seem to keep slipping through your fingers, take a step back and run a "Buckets of Time" analysis on your work or personal life. This tool will provide all the data you need to pinpoint any adjustments or changes you need to make in your roles, goals, Habits, and schedule to support your continuing growth in Habitual Greatness.

7. **Schedule Yourself for Greatness:** The single most important change you can make in your life is to schedule it effectively, then keep to your word, and stick to your schedule. Keep track of your life and commitments in one universal place, whether in an electronic or paper format, so that nothing falls through the cracks. Reschedule missed actions without criticizing yourself—no worries—learn to hold yourself accountable and to identify the Habits in the way!

8. **Employ the Simplest and Most Effective To-Do System:** As with your schedule, maintain a single to-do receptacle. Carry it with you at all times. And initiate a regular end-of-day and end-of week review to move all incomplete items from your list directly into your schedule,

giving each task a date and time for completion. Then watch your productivity soar!

9. **Prepare for Interruptions and Banish Distractions:** Accept that interruptions and distractions are inevitable and part of life. The key is to monitor their sources and quantity and keep them under control. If you spot any Limiting Beliefs or Habits as their sources, do whatever it takes to Shift to their counterparts. Use the other tips in this chapter to corral the rest.

10. **Carve Out Solitary Work Blocks with No Interruptions:** Organize your daily work schedule around large blocks of time where you can focus for extended periods on taking your most important initiatives and projects forward.

11. **Nail Down Your Stop Doing List:** Support your schedule and top priorities by creating a list of those things you are going to stop doing—such as old tasks that no longer contribute to your goals, projects that are better delegated, commitments that were wrong to commit to, and Limiting Beliefs and Habits you are taking Action to eliminate. Then schedule and execute the relevant Actions—including contacting anyone who may be affected by your decisions.

12. **Dream Up Your Start Doing List:** Leverage your new productivity and success structure Habits by applying them to even more of your desired objectives and dreams. Make a list of passions to explore, exciting things to finish, new projects to begin, skills you want to learn, courses to take, trips to make, relationships you'd like to initiate, and

PUTTING IT ALL TOGETHER

Peak Life Habits to master. Then work them into your schedule and follow through with Right Action. Savor your new feelings of passion and enthusiasm for life!

13. **Take On the "Confrontation With Being Complete Habit":** Refuse to allow self-defeating drives masquerading as independence and spontaneity or deeper fears of completion, failure, or success rob you of the joy of achievement! Root these Limiting Habits out at their source and Shift to their Peak Life Habit counterparts.

14. **Practice Reverse Timeline Scheduling:** Support yourself in fulfilling simple and complex, short or long-term objectives by using Imagineering to determine all the steps you will take and milestones you will reach to complete them. Then, working backwards from your desired completion all the way to your initiation date, schedule each Action step in your planner.

15. **Build Teamwork by Mastering the Art of Delegation:** Appreciate how much you rely on others to help you achieve your goals, fulfill your intentions, live your purpose, and manifest your dreams. Practice the "Teamwork Habit" to build trust and camaraderie in your daily life and work and master the eight-step process of the "Effective Delegation Habit" to empower your teams in catapulting from one *Positively Inspiring Success* to the next!

16. **Be Great at Your Job!:** Play daily at being a peak performer, modeling standout behavior, and achieving top-notch results. Use and strengthen every Peak Life Habit in your arsenal, and develop new ones on a consistent

basis. Relish the integrity of doing and being your best—Habitually Great—every day on the job!

WHAT TO DO NEXT

Often when people discover new breakthroughs, they envision their life changing profoundly for the better, and then something happens—life interferes. This is where your Habitually Great preemptive visioning comes in. Step outside of that predicament and into your great life.

Here's what to do. There are two sections upcoming; one, if you want to advance the growth and peak performance in your organization or workplace, then turn to page 132-133. And if you want a personal life with even greater joy and fulfillment, then keep on reading.

What To Do Next—In Your Life
Take Action To Be Habitually Great!

If you want to change your personal life, if you are ready to truly master your Habits and own your destiny, then you'll want to consider the programs below. Find where you are on the chart and take the next step that's best for you.

IF YOU WANT	→	Select...	→	AT
To rapidly and permanently shift the experience of your vitality, relationships, fulfillment, self-esteem, wellness, and career	→	Habitually Great Coaching	→	HabituallyGreat.com/lifecoaching
High-impact and interactive group learning, virtually or physically	→	Habitually Great Events	→	HabituallyGreat.com/events
To move at your own pace on your own schedule	→	Habitually Great Programs	→	HabituallyGreat.com/programs

What To Do Next—At Work

Individually and Organizationally Take Action To Be Habitually Great!

Habitually Great professional programs are offered both virtually and onsite. These programs help to create a deeply fulfilling work environment, peak performing teams, and profound alignment with the corporate mission. Executive coaching, workshops and trainings, onsite coach training, and keynote speaking are several of the programs offered. Select the next step for yourself and/or your organization!

WHAT TO DO NEXT

IF YOU WANT	→	Select…	→	AT
Peak-performing executives and managers	→	Habitually Great Executive Coaching	→	HabituallyGreat.com/execcoaching
To create lasting breakthroughs in culture, communication, results, teamwork, accountability	→	Habitually Great Corporate Workshops/Trainings	→	HabituallyGreat.com/corporate
To leverage internal trainers and presenters for leadership development at your organization	→	Habitually Great Internal Coach Training	→	HabituallyGreat.com/coachtraining
To provide an interactive, high-impact, one-time or introductory experience of Habitually Great transformation	→	Habitually Great Keynotes	→	HabituallyGreat.com/keynotes

HABITUALLY GREAT APPENDICES

Appendix A: Peak Life Habits

Peak Life Habits are positive, Action-oriented Habits that you deploy to preemptively circumvent your Limiting Habits. As you consciously choose these Habits you advance directly to the joys and successes you truly desire; to your greatness. The Peak Life Habits listed below are those specifically found in this book. You can find the complete list as well as a free resource file with definitions of several Habits at www.habituallygreat.com/resources.

- ☐ Accountability Habit
- ☐ Acknowledgement Habit
- ☐ Acting As If Habit
- ☐ Always Learning Habit
- ☐ Apology Habit
- ☐ Authentic Habit
- ☐ Being Appropriate Habit
- ☐ Being Great At My Job Habit
- ☐ Being In Action Habit
- ☐ Being Inviting/Enrolling Habit
- ☐ Being Unstoppable Habit
- ☐ Believe In Myself Habit
- ☐ Communicate Accountabilities Habit
- ☐ Compassionate Habit
- ☐ Completion Habit
- ☐ Courage Habit
- ☐ Courage & Humility Habit
- ☐ Create My Destiny (vs. Fate) Habit
- ☐ Creating A Powerful Future Habit
- ☐ Detachment Habit
- ☐ Determined To Succeed Habit
- ☐ Discipline Habit
- ☐ Effective Delegation Habit
- ☐ Emotional Fortitude Habit
- ☐ Empowered Language Habit
- ☐ Empowering People Habit
- ☐ Excellence Habit
- ☐ Express Enthusiastic Agreement Habit
- ☐ Express Kindness & Love As A Verb Habit
- ☐ Feeling Good Habit
- ☐ Focus & Clarity Habit

HABITUALLY GREAT APPENDICES

- ☐ Ground Truth Reality Habit
- ☐ Healthy Exercise Habit
- ☐ Healthy Trust Habit
- ☐ Healthy Vulnerability Habit
- ☐ Humility Habit
- ☐ I Can Do It Habit
- ☐ I Remember Habit
- ☐ I'm Organized Habit
- ☐ I'm Worthy Habit
- ☐ Integrity Habit
- ☐ Keep Both Feet In Habit
- ☐ Keep The Faith Habit
- ☐ Keeping My Word Habit
- ☐ Kindness Habit
- ☐ Laughter Habit
- ☐ Leading By Example Habit
- ☐ Learning From My Failures Habit
- ☐ Lightening Up Habit
- ☐ Living In Reality Habit
- ☐ Living Powerfully Habit
- ☐ Making Powerful Choices Habit
- ☐ Modeling Well Habit
- ☐ No More Excuses Habit
- ☐ No Regrets Habit
- ☐ On Time Habit
- ☐ Open Heart Habit
- ☐ Patience Habit
- ☐ Pattern Interrupt Habit
- ☐ Persistence Habit
- ☐ Playing Big Habit
- ☐ Positive Results Language Habit
- ☐ Power Scheduling Habit
- ☐ Power (vs. Force) Habit
- ☐ Preempt Your Interruptions Habit
- ☐ Preemptive Habit
- ☐ Proactive Habit
- ☐ Putting Myself First Habit
- ☐ Resolving Past Issues Habit
- ☐ Resolving Prior Commitments Habit
- ☐ Responding (vs. Reacting) Habit
- ☐ Right Action Habit
- ☐ Right Action Momentum Habit
- ☐ Rigor Habit
- ☐ Saying No Authentically Habit
- ☐ Saying Yes Powerfully Habit
- ☐ Schedule My Relationships Habit
- ☐ Seeing What's Right Habit
- ☐ Seek First To Understand Habit
- ☐ Self-Accountability Habit
- ☐ Self-Love Habit

HABITUALLY GREAT PRODUCTIVITY & TIME MANAGEMENT

- ☐ Teamwork Habit
- ☐ The Right Time Is Right Now Habit
- ☐ Time Is Just Time Habit
- ☐ Trusting Others Habit
- ☐ U-Turning My Finger Habit
- ☐ Walk My Talk Habit
- ☐ Fill In: _____
- ☐ Fill In: _____

Appendix B: Limiting Habits

These Habits limit your greatness and interfere with the goals and successes you desire in your life. Don't worry if you have an entire column's worth (and all it takes is one to interfere with your life's desires); many great and happy people started this process with that surprising awakening! The Limiting Habits listed below are those specifically found in this book. You can find the complete list as well as a free resource file with definitions of several Habits at www.habituallygreat.com/resources.

- ☐ Annoyed/Annoying Habit
- ☐ Avoid Accountability Habit
- ☐ Avoid Authority Habit
- ☐ Can't Say No Habit
- ☐ Confrontation With Success Habit
- ☐ Cut & Run Habit
- ☐ Difficult to Deal With Habit
- ☐ Disempowering People Habit
- ☐ Distraction/Interruption Habit
- ☐ Distress Habit
- ☐ Do It Myself Habit
- ☐ Doing It My Way Habit
- ☐ Domination & Control Habit
- ☐ Drama Habit
- ☐ Every Other Monther Habit
- ☐ Excuses Habit
- ☐ Frustration Habit
- ☐ Good Person Habit
- ☐ Hard on Myself Habit
- ☐ I Can Do It Better & Faster Habit
- ☐ I Don't Trust Habit
- ☐ I'm Not Good Enough Habit
- ☐ I'm Not Great Habit
- ☐ I'm Not Safe Habit
- ☐ I'm Not Worthy Habit
- ☐ I'm Right Habit
- ☐ Logic & Justify Habit
- ☐ Looking Good Habit
- ☐ Need to be Needed Habit
- ☐ Making People Feel Bad Habit
- ☐ Obsess Habit
- ☐ Open Door Habit
- ☐ Over-Think Habit
- ☐ Overwhelm Habit
- ☐ Perfectionist Habit
- ☐ Procrastination Habit
- ☐ Regret Habit
- ☐ Resentment Habit
- ☐ Resignation Habit
- ☐ Seeing What's Wrong Habit

HABITUALLY GREAT APPENDICES

- ☐ Resignation Habit
- ☐ Seeing What's Wrong Habit
- ☐ Self-Sabotage Habit
- ☐ Shortcut Habit
- ☐ Skepticism Habit
- ☐ Struggle Habit
- ☐ Stuck In My Assumptions Habit
- ☐ There's No Time Habit
- ☐ This Isn't 'It' Habit
- ☐ Victim Habit

Appendix C
Shifting Limiting Habits
to
Peak Life Habits

Here is a handy "Shifting Chart" with *Peak Life Habits* that are effective replacements for Limiting Habits. Use this chart as a powerful guide and also enjoy selecting *Peak Life Habits* that you custom tailor for your great life!

LIMITING HABITS	Shift to	PEAK LIFE HABITS
Annoyed/Annoying Habit	→	*U-Turning My Finger Habit* *Compassion Habit*
Avoid Accountability Habit	→	*Accountability Habit* *The Right Time Is Right Now Habit*
Avoid Authority Habit	→	*Healthy Vulnerability Habit* *Accountability Habit*
Can't Say No Habit	→	*Saying No Authentically Habit* *Putting Myself First Habit*
Confrontation With Success Habit	→	*Success Habit* *Believe In Myself Habit*

LIMITING HABITS	Shift to	PEAK LIFE HABITS
Cut & Run Habit	→	Right Action Momentum Habit Persistence Habit
Difficult to Deal With Habit	→	Teamwork Habit Being Appropriate Habit
Disempowering People Habit	→	Empowering People Habit Trusting Others Habit
Distraction/Interruption Habit	→	Focus & Clarity Habit Completion Habit
Distress Habit	→	Lightening Up Habit Seeing What's Right Habit
Do It Myself Habit	→	Open Heart Habit Teamwork Habit
Doing It My Way Habit	→	Seek First to Understand Habit Teamwork Habit
Domination & Control Habit	→	Great Listener Habit Power (vs. Force) Habit
Drama Habit	→	Lightening Up Habit Being Appropriate Habit
Every Other Monther	→	Accountability Habit Determined To Succeed Habit

LIMITING HABITS	Shift to	PEAK LIFE HABITS
Excuses Habit	→	Completion Habit Apology Habit
Frustration Habit	→	Patience Habit Detachment Habit
Good Person Habit	→	Saying No Authentically Habit Ground Truth Reality Habit
Hard On Myself Habit	→	Lightening Up Habit Seeing What's Right Habit
I Can Do It Better & Faster Habit	→	Effective Delegation Habit Teamwork Habit
I Don't Trust Habit	→	Open Heart Habit Teamwork Habit
I'm Not Good Enough Habit	→	I'm Worthy Habit Being Unstoppable Habit
I'm Not Great Habit	→	Believe In Myself Habit Greatness Habit
I'm Not Safe Habit	→	Courage Habit Emotional Fortitude Habit
I'm Not Worthy Habit	→	Greatness In Action Habit No More Excuses Habit

HABITUALLY GREAT APPENDICES

LIMITING HABITS	Shift to	PEAK LIFE HABITS
I'm Right Habit	→	Leading By Example Habit U-Turn My Finger Habit
Logic & Justify Habit	→	Authentic Habit Ground Truth Reality Habit
Looking Good Habit	→	Humility Habit Healthy Vulnerability Habit
Making People Feel Bad Habit	→	Lightening Up Habit Effective Delegation Habit
Needing To Be Needed	→	I Am Good Enough Habit Stop Doing Habit
Obsess Habit	→	Detachment Habit Patience Habit
Open Door Habit	→	Saying No Authentically Habit Power Scheduling Habit
Overwhelm Habit	→	Saying No Authentically Habit Discipline Habit
Over-Think Habit	→	Greatness In Action Habit Lightening Up Habit

LIMITING HABITS	Shift to	PEAK LIFE HABITS
Perfectionist Habit	→	Playing Big Habit Right Time Is Right Now Habit
Procrastination Habit	→	Accountability Habit Right Time Is Right Now Habit
Regret Habit	→	Learning From My Failures Habit Courage Habit
Resentment Habit	→	Compassion Habit U-Turning My Finger Habit
Resignation Habit	→	Playing Big Habit Living Powerfully Habit
Seeing What's Wrong Habit	→	Seeing What's Right Habit Lightening Up Habit
Self-Sabotage Habit	→	Pattern Interrupt Habit Squash The Wiggle Habit
Skepticism Habit	→	Believe In Myself Habit Being Unstoppable Habit
Struggle Habit	→	Lightening Up Habit Success Habit

LIMITING HABITS	Shift to	PEAK LIFE HABITS
Shortcut Habit	→	Discipline Habit Patience Habit
Stuck In My Assumptions Habit	→	Always Learning Habit Great Listener Habit
There's No Time Habit	→	Power Scheduling Habit Saying No Authentically Habit
This Isn't It Habit	→	Seeing What's Right Habit Seek First To Understand Habit
Victim Habit	→	Living Powerfully Habit Accountability Habit

About Mark Weinstein

Mark Weinstein is the author of *Habitually Great Productivity & Time Management: Master The Framework of Your Life,* and the Founder and CEO of Habitually Great®, Inc., (www.habituallygreat.com) a firm specializing in personal development and organizational greatness through keynote speaking, leadership events, coaching and training programs. Mark is also the author of the full suite of Habitually Great books, including the award-winning book, *Habitually Great: Master Your Habits, Own Your Destiny, Habitually Great Communication: Master The Power of Your Words,* and the *Habitually Great Companion Workbook Series.*

Habitually Great: Master Your Habits, Own Your Destiny has been endorsed by the esteemed Dr. Stephen R. Covey, read by thousands of people, and received a Finalist Award in the "Motivational" category from the Indie Book Awards. Mark is often a guest on talk programs and has been a featured writer in leadership publications, such as *Leader to Leader,* an award-winning journal.

Over the past 30 years, Mark has studied contemporary thought leaders, including Deepak Chopra, Jim Collins, Dr. Stephen R. Covey, Frances Hesselbein, Dr. Wayne W. Dyer, T. Harv Eker, Robert Fritz, Marshall Goldsmith, Harville Hendrix, Esther Hicks, Patrick Lencioni, Anthony Robbins, Maggie Victor, Marianne Williamson, and many others.

"Regardless of how engaging, how inspiring, and how insightful so many books and programs are in the moment," Mark says, "come Monday morning we often revert back to our old habits. Insights disappear; habits don't." To resolve this quandary, Mark developed the Peak Life Habits methodology, which is the cornerstone of *Habitually Great* books and programs.

Mark earned his MBA from the Anderson School at the University of California, Los Angeles, with concentrations in Strategic Market Management and Organizational Process. He earned his BA with College Honors, Thesis Honors, and Honors in Sociology from the University of California, Santa Cruz. This was the genesis of his interest in human socialization and its impact on personal achievement.

Mark has traveled extensively around the world. He has climbed peaks as high as 18,500 feet in Nepal. He was at the Berlin Wall and inside East Germany the day the wall came down. He is a graduate of both the Skip Barber and Spring Mountain Advanced Racing Schools and has driven on the Estoril Racetrack in Portugal at speeds exceeding 160 mph. Mark was also a Silver Medalist in tennis at the US Olympic Committee's 2005 State Games of America.

During Mark's career, he has been the CEO of a leading Web 1.0 social network Internet company (supergroups.com); has served as the Chairman of the New Mexico State Board of Accountancy; has taught on the graduate business level as an Adjunct Professor at the University of New Mexico's

ABOUT MARK WEINSTEIN

Anderson School of Management; and before attending graduate school, he was a leading automotive journalist, testing new cars on racetracks around the world, while writing in magazines and newspapers. Mark is the founder and CEO of Sgrouples.com.

Mark Weinstein and the Habitually Great staff conduct speaking engagements, keynotes, life and executive coaching, workshops, and seminars around the United States for many individuals, conferences, and organizations. The Habitually Great corporate client list has included Wells Fargo Bank, FedEx Kinko's, Coldwell Banker Legacy, ADP, American Red Cross, Hyatt Regency, and many others. Our company maintains a distinct cadre of individual and corporate clients, from Hollywood to New York to Kansas. All have a common focus: Greatness.

Let us help you be Great!

You can contact Mark at author@habituallygreat.com.